# JUMPin2it! BREAKTHRU MARKETING GUIDE



ISBN 978-1-7776899-8-8 Paperback

ISBN 978-1-7776899-7-1 eBook

ISBN 978-1-7776899-8-8 Audio

## DEDICATION

To our mothers, who taught us the value of hard work, perseverance, and the power of believing in ourselves. Your unwavering support and endless encouragement have been the foundation of our journey.

To our children, your patience, understanding, and love have been our driving force.

This book is also dedicated to all those who dream of building a successful business and strive to be the best they can be. To those who are determined to make a difference through their businesses or by passionately marketing the products and services they believe in—we honor your dedication and drive. This book is for you, with all our love and gratitude.

## Table of Contents

# LIST OF ABBREVIATIONS

The following table explains abbreviations used throughout the book. The page on which each one is defined or first used is also given.

| Abbreviation | Meaning |
| --- | --- |
| API | Application Programming Interface |
| B2B | Business-to-Business |
| B2C | Business-to-Consumer |
| BOTF | Bottom Of The Funnel |
| CMA | Canadian Marketing Association |
| CMS | Content Management System |
| CPC | Cost Per Click |
| CPM | Cost Per Thousand (Impression)/Cost Per Mille |
| CPV | Cost Per View |
| CRM | Customer Relation Management |
| CRO | Conversion Rate Optimization |
| CTR | Click-Through Rate |
| HTML | HyperText Markup Language |
| IT | Information Technology |
| KPI | Key Performance Indicator |
| MarTech | Marketing Technology |

| MOTF | Middle Of The Funnel |
|------|----------------------|
| MROI | Marketing Return On Investment |
| MTA | Multi-Touch Attribution |
| PPC | Pay Per Click |
| PR | Public Relations |
| RFP | Request For Proposal |
| ROI | Return On Investment |
| SaaS | Software As A Service |
| SEO | Search Engine Optimization |
| SERP | Search Engine Results Page/Search Engine Ranking Pages |
| SFA | Sales Force Automation |
| SME | Small Medium Enterprise |
| SOV | Share Of Voice |
| SSL | Secure Sockets Layer |
| TOTF | Top Of The Sales Funnel |
| URL | Uniform Resource Locator |
| USP | Unique Selling Proposition |
| UVP | Unique Value Proposition |

## FOREWORD

A practical and detailed guide that takes you through every step of business development and marketing strategy. If you want to reap the value this book offers, take out your post-it notes and highlighters and prepare to embark on a series of exploratory questions that will help you define your goals, understand and appreciate your audience, articulate your value and plan your go-to-market strategy.

Gabrielle and Anita have generously consolidated and made available to their readers many decades worth of study and practical experience. Use this guide, with the accompanying digital playbook, as your personal win strategy toolkit. The process is logical and simple, but requires time, commitment and honesty.

Sales and Marketing leaders may want to organize a series of dynamic workshops with their team to go through each step of the guide. A valuable exercise if entering a new line of business or launching new products, or simply looking for a way to refresh current sales and marketing approaches to reflect new competitive or market dynamics.

Solo entrepreneurs will find comfort in these pages. You will feel supported by strategic advisors asking you pointed questions to make sure your strategy, plans and actions are destined to succeed.

As you embark on the next few pages, do not sit back and relax. Save that for other leisure reading. Sit up,

fueled and energized, alone or with a team, and be prepared to think, pause, write, erase and write again. If you put in as much passion and attention in reading this guide as the authors have put into writing it, your gains will be meaningful and measurable.
This is not a sprint – it is a marathon. Make it your personal best.

Lisa Azzuolo
Marketing Executive


## INTRODUCTION

In today's competitive landscape, your business's survival depends on your ability to attract and retain customers. To effectively persuade buyers to choose your products or services, you need more than just a persistent salesperson. A robust, cost-efficient marketing strategy is essential to avoid wasting resources on plans that don't work. This is your fast-track guide to becoming a marketing genius.

Before diving into strategy planning or campaign development, take the time to read this guide. You'll find it to be a valuable investment. With over 40 years of combined marketing experience in driving business growth, we share the critical elements that deliver immediate and long-term results without unnecessary spending.

Whether you are a senior marketer, executive, or entrepreneur, this book equips you with proven processes, plans, to make your vision of a successful business a prosperous reality. The **"JUMPin2it! Breakthru Marketing Guide**" outlines the essential building blocks for fast wins to lasting success, whether you're a large enterprise, a mid-sized company, or a start-up. While the scope of your services, resources, and go-to-market plans may differ, the foundational steps remain consistent.

Through detailed strategies, targeted questions, and practical scenarios, this guide focuses on the most impactful levers to enhance your marketing and sales efforts. As you fast-track guide to turning your vision into action, we'll take you through the entire persuasion process—from building awareness to securing sales to creating brand ambassadors. Along the way, you will uncover the most cost-effective marketing opportunities that will position you to have a prosperous business.

This book serves as your roadmap for making marketing the best investment for your business. When every element is strategically aligned, you not only create a predictable, repeatable, and cost-effective sales funnel but also lay a solid foundation for sustainable business growth.

But we don't stop there. The cost of acquiring, retaining, and expanding your customer base is crucial to scalability. We'll share strategies to keep your marketing costs low and ensure you stay focused on maximizing your Marketing Return on Investment (MROI).

Consider this guide your ultimate resource, packed with strategies, plans, and tools proven successful across industries. You'll want to refer to it often as you expand into new markets, introduce new business lines, or launch new products. With this fast-track guide, you'll have the tools and insights needed to navigate today's complex and competitive business landscape, to achieve fast wins and long-term success.


**Gabrielle Hailmann**

As President of 360 Integral Marketing, she is committed to driving business success through cost-effective, performance-based marketing strategies. With over 20 years of expertise, she specializes in creating integrated sales ecosystems and digital

CRM programs that deliver measurable results at every touch point with the buyer.

Gabrielle has a proven track record of launching small businesses, accelerating the growth of mid-sized companies, and spearheading advancements in digital lead generation and marketing automation. Her expertise, developed through leadership roles at RBC Royal Bank, Rogers Communications, American Express, and ADP Canada, has made her a recognized authority in the field. In 2010, she was honored as one of the top ten women in Direct Marketing by Direct Marketing Magazine.

## Anita Booth

Anita Booth is a seasoned marketing and communications leader recognized for driving growth and innovation across startups and established businesses. Currently, she serves as Vice President of Marketing & Communications, for a global organization dedicated to promoting gender parity in the financial services industry.

Anita is one of the hosts of the Jumpin2it Podcast, which inspires others to spark change through the sharing of insights and ideas. Known as the idea alchemist, she is passionate about empowering professionals and inspiring transformative growth. With impactful tenures with large financial institutions, and years helping small businesses, Anita has a proven track record of delivering outstanding marketing strategies, brand transformations, and digital innovation.

## JUMPin2it SECTION I - LAYING THE GROUNDWORK

The Essential Step to Marketing Mastery

"Strategy is about making choices, trade-offs; it's about choosing to be different." Michael Porter, Author & Academic

Strategy is the blueprint for achieving your goals. Effective strategizing requires open-mindedness, perceptiveness, and the foresight to anticipate future trends. In this section, we guide you through strategies that serve as the foundation for your business, brand, and marketing efforts—critical steps to ensure you don't waste time and money on ineffective plans. We also provide insights to help you distinguish between strategies that will succeed and those that may fall short.

Never underestimate the value of a well-defined strategy. Although it can take time to map out where you want your business to go and how to get there, this investment is crucial. In a rapidly changing environment, time is a precious resource, but skipping essential steps can be even more costly. Becoming proficient in marketing starts with asking the right questions, making decisions based on research, logic, and well-calculated assumptions.

Even experienced marketers can sometimes miss key elements of the strategy puzzle. To help you avoid these pitfalls and move closer to marketing genius, here's a quick review:

## Business Strategy

A business strategy requires a more in-depth review of the competitive landscape, the market trends, the organizational structure and scale, cash flow, technology and more.

## Brand Strategy

A brand strategy focuses on bringing your business strategy to life. A brand strategy includes brand attributes, a unique value proposition, vision, mission, and values.

## Marketing Strategy

The last piece of the puzzle is the marketing strategy. Marketing is about actively promoting and selling a product or service. It's putting the right product/service in the right place, at the right price, at the right time with the right conversation. It moves and activates buyers at different stages of the sales funnel.

The marketing strategy is shaped by the business and brand strategy and more tactical in nature. At this stage you are taking a deeper dive into the business's products and services. Some steps might even seem a bit repetitive, however when you drill down on your business offering, another layer of analysis is required. The marketing strategy plays a big role in developing effective sales funnels, which we explore further in section II.

In this section **Be Strategic**, you will be tasked to uncover the needs for business growth and success. With the high failure rate of businesses, there's no guarantee a strategy will meet all expectations and goals. But when you keep an open mind, and gather the business intelligence to make calculated decisions, it dramatically increases your chances for success.

## Start with a Business Strategy

**Building the Foundation for Business Growth**

A business strategy sets the stage for business growth. Whether you are an entrepreneur, a small business owner or the CEO of a fortune 500 company, the responsibility falls on you and the senior team to define, develop, and execute the business strategy. It needs to include achievable goals on how to stay ahead of the competition, build your brand and be profitable.

An effective strategy contains five key elements that are not mutually exclusive.  They are as follows:

1. **Strategic Focus** – start with the business goals. What products, distribution channels, market segments and geographies do you want to take-on?
2. **Differentiators** – how will you set yourself apart from your competition? Look at your image, pricing, product selection and services.
3. **Drivers** – how will you grow, strategic alliances, licensing, product development, acquisition?
4. **Positioning** – how will you advance; will it be by product or image and what order?
5. **Economics** – how will you be more profitable? Lower costs, premium services, or premium pricing?

When building a holistic strategy, everyone in the organization can stay focused; making roles, responsibilities, structure, and resources work together to achieve the business goals set out in the strategy.

Answering 12 Strategy Questions

As you seek to build your strategy, here are questions that will help you establish the foundation for building your brand.

## 1. What is the vision for your company?

What is your vision? What does your product or service offer your customers, stakeholders, and employees? Does it have an effect in their lives?

## 2. How will you make the business grow?

What are the organization's plans for growth and what are the specific growth targets? Are there ways to grow through acquisition, organically, expansion into new markets, acquiring market share or developing new products?

## 3. What is the core strength of your business?

Describe its greatest strengths. What is unique about your business? Is the status quo being challenged? What is working, can you do more of it and how you can do it better?

## 4. Who will you sell your products and services to?

Where will you get the most sales? Who will be your loyal customers? Remember the 80/20 rule, 80% of your sales will come from 20% of your customers. How can you describe them?  Have you segmented them by high value versus low value customers? Can they be grouped in a meaningful way to communicate to, sell and service?

**5. What are your key differentiators, your Unique Value Proposition (UVP)?**
Why will your customers choose to buy from you and not the competition?  Is it price, quality, value, convenience, ease of use, uniqueness?

**6. What is not working?**

Identity what is not working or what isn't creating value. These could be anything from an unpromising customer segment you are pursuing to an internal process that decreases agility. Challenge the status quo. Do not be afraid to call out the obstacles in your path.

**7. What are the biggest roadblocks?**

What are the biggest threats to organizational performance, both external and internal? Can they be listed and prioritized? Which are most detrimental to the business?

## 8. What are the disruptions your business could face?

What are the disruptions your business faces, whether it's the competition or the release of game-changing technology? These are the sudden shifts that could change everything. What will you do about them? Can you start any disruptions of your own?

## 9. What can be improved upon?

How can you improve the products or services you bring to the market? Are there enhancements needed to block competitor plays, adjust to market changes, or consumer preferences?

## 10. What do your customers want now and in the future?

What do your customers want from the business today? Will this change in the next five years? Is there a need for market research? What are the customer needs today and how those might change in the next 5-years?

## 11. How do your employees play into your strategy?

Do you have the right team to help bring your products and services to market? Think through what the organization does well in this domain and what may be missing. Your employees can be your best brand ambassadors, it's important to include them in bringing your product to life in the marketplace.

**12. How do shareholders fit into your business strategy?**

Are there plans to take the business public at some point? Is there a need for investors? Will it be cash flow, stock appreciation, or another growth goal?

By answering these questions, you will create the framework for the business strategy and will crystalize the goals the business is looking to achieve. Building and filling the sales funnel needs to fit into the growth targets of the business. Everyone in the organization must connect with the strategy and incorporate it as part of their day-to-day activities.

# Build a Successful Brand

**Building the Foundation for Business Growth**

When creating a brand, it's important to let your buyers know what to expect from your company and its products and services. It distinguishes the business and its product lines from its competitors.

A strong brand builds buyer preference, shortens the sales cycle, makes your consumer less price sensitive and drives referrals. Your brand, when well communicated, lets customers know what you are about and what you represent. This includes but not limited to the creation of a name, symbols, imagery, designs, messaging, and a positive user experience.

When a brand is well-defined and established, it gains trust and familiarity, which gives you a competitive edge, repeat customers and increased sales revenue!

## Steps in Building a Successful Brand

Let's talk about the elements required for building a successful brand. You may have already addressed a few when building the business strategy. Review below the questions, to make sure you have things covered.

1. What is the vision, mission, and values of the company?

2. What are the business goals and objectives?

3. Who are the target audiences, can you group them into meaningful segments and buyer personas?

4. What problem are you trying to solve?

5. What solutions do you have that will solve their problem?

6. How is your product/service offering different from your competitors' – what is your unique value proposition?

7. Where do your audiences like to hang out?

8. What would you tell them about your business products/services?

9. What is the best way to reach your target audience(s) to tell them about your product offering?

10. How do you want your brand to look and feel and how will that translate into advertising and messaging?

## Your Target Audience – Defining Your Segments and Personas

To strengthen your business, your brand needs to be communicated to the right stakeholders with the right message. How you define your current and future customers is by segmentation and persona creation.

### Segments

Segmentation helps determine and quantify the demand for your brand or product in the marketplace. It's based on grouping together customers with commonalities that are meaningful and relevant for marketing, selling, and servicing. Customers can be grouped by demographics, firmographics, interests, life stages, geographies, race, opinions, risk level and buying behaviour - combining any or all of these. Marketing messaging, content strategy, and product targeting all need to be aligned with each segment and be supported by your brand strategy. Leverage research, data analysis, surveys, and sales transactions for creating your customer segments.

## Personas

Personas differ from segments as they are more on an individual level, where you paint the picture of who your ideal buyers are, more precisely what they want or need in their life. It considers their values and goals.

Segments are used to attract buyers to your brand. Personas help determine personality, what interests them to buy and how to motivate them to convert. As personas will play an important part of building your persuasion sequence, let's take a deeper look into how to create them.

Mapping out the user profiles or pathways to consumption is an ideal way to isolate and build a persona of the ideal buyer. When you build out a persona of your customer, you will not only understand the type of content that will resonate with them, but you'll also identify ways in which they will consume the content. You will know with a higher degree of certainty how to speak more directly and effectively to your customers in the places they're likely to be, through the channels they're most likely to use and with language that's most likely to resonate with them.

Personas don't just help you crystalize your brand messaging, they help to qualify leads, inform product development, develop creative that resonates, and creates more effective alignment with your sales teams. According to experts, when you take the time to understand the persona of your buyer, it increases customer retention by 5%, and can grow profits by 25%-95% [i]

How do you build a persona? Easy - find out more about your target buyer and write it down.

Do some research on the topics below and you'll begin to build a clear picture of what they look like.

Refer to your segmentation. What does your customer look like, male/female, age, education, income, marital status, children, friends?

Look at other buyers of a similar product/service and see if there are any pain points those products/services are trying to fill.

Are there any patterns? Are there any common triggers that push them to buy a specific product? What is the pain point the product is looking to solve? What is their end goal?

**Create the persona**. Do you have a picture in mind of what this buyer looks like now? Give them a name and face. Find images and traits of this person and bring them to life on paper. Caricatures are a great and fun way to build personas. Give them a favourite saying, show the car they like to drive, and even the coffee they like to drink. The more details of the person, the better equipped you'll be to connect with them.

Create key messages that speak directly to their pain points. When you build out key messages, they become part of your play book which is a critical part of any marketing plan.

Segments and personas are both important. Together they give you a comprehensive picture for building out your brand strategy, marketing plans and filling your sales funnel!

## Create a Marketing Strategy that Drives Results

## Building the Foundation for Business Growth

Now that you've completed the Business Strategy and flushed out the components of the Brand Strategy, it's time to look at the Marketing Strategy. A Marketing Strategy represents the dynamics of the organization and the marketplace. It provides a compass towards the direction the company will take to build a profitable and sustainable business.

Developing a marketing strategy starts with the time and effort in understanding the internal and external influencing factors that drive sales. Experience, data, technology, and know-how will be needed to identify and quantify the marketing opportunities that will fill your sales funnel today and longer term.

The Marketing Strategy, once complete will be the last stage prior to planning and selecting tactics for acquiring new customers and retaining existing ones. The next few pages outlines what the Marketing Strategy needs to include.


## Competitive Analysis

If you don't know your competition, it's likely your potential buyers will.  With all the information on the Internet, buyers are more informed and expect you to be too. Gathering information will help you better place yourself against the competition and identify gaps and opportunities to win over your buyers and deal with market uncertainties. Below are the steps on how to complete an analysis to understand your business's competitive landscape.

## SWOT (Strengths, Weakness, Opportunities, Threats) Analysis

With a SWOT analysis there four areas of analysis to complete: your specific strengths, weaknesses, opportunities, and threats within your market. If there are areas that are particularly notable, expound upon those.

- **Strengths** (internal advantages, what you are already doing well, your competitive edge)

- **Weaknesses** (internal inefficiencies, areas
  the organization is falling behind the
  competition on or is lacking in resources)
- **Opportunities** (external areas within the
  marketplace where the competition is weak,
  and your business has potential. Using the
  PEST (political, economic, social,
  technological analysis to cover all bases)
- **Threats** (external area where the competition
  is strong or there is a market trend with the
  potential to harm your organization. Again,
  use the PEST analysis here)

## Target Market

In this section provide a synopsis of your segments
and buyer personas that you completed as part of
the brand exercise. Highlight your key segments and
personas primary and secondary targets, as well as
the types of buyers you want to avoid. Consider
influencers, end users and ambassadors.

## Customers' Buying Cycle

Through primary and secondary research discover
how, when, where and why they buy. This is crucial
to your strategy. To sell to them, you need to
determine where they are shopping, when and why.

Your unique selling proposition is the essence of what makes your product or service better than your competitors. It needs to be clearly defined and easily communicated to your target audience and across integrated communications. The importance of a well crafted USP, especially online should never be overlooked as it is a key driver in convincing potential buyers to purchase your products and services.

## Brand Building

Discuss how your brand is currently perceived in the marketplace and any adjustments or improvements required. How do you plan to increase visibility and recognition as well as address any reputation challenges you might encounter?

Marketing strategies have a longer lifespan than individual marketing plans as they contain value propositions and key elements of a company's brand. While marketing plans expand on the logistical details of specific campaigns, marketing strategies cover big picture thinking as follows:

- It pushes you to understand the driving forces in the industry and which competitors you are up against

- Outlines the company's situation with reference to the internal and the external environment
- Includes proper situation analysis – the background and foundation for the strategic direction
- It addresses the resources needed to build out and execute an effective and cost-efficient marketing plan to grow your business
- It will identify marketing opportunities that are the best fit for the organization based on brand, resources, and potential profitability

In answering the Marketing Strategy questions below, they'll provide the greatest impact to the development of your marketing plans:

- Who are your customers?
- Who are your competitors?

- How is your product/service offering different than your competitors' – what is your unique value proposition?
- What are your 4Ps, your products, pricing, promotions, and places?
- What are your sales channels, will you be selling through eCommerce, direct sales, brick and mortars or a combination?
- How much budget will be invested in the marketing strategy for acquiring, retaining, and growing your customer base?
- Every business in start-up or growth mode requires a technology infrastructure. What tools are you investing in to improve the customer experience and provide invaluable intel on your customer base?
- How will the other departments support the growth targets? Are the call centres, customer service reps, sales teams, IT, and warehouse personnel professionally trained and staffed to handle an increase in sales?

When reviewing your marketing strategy, ensure you have adequately answered the questions above. Then you can align your goals with a marketing budget.

# Align Your Goals to a Marketing Budget

After you've completed the strategy work, and your big picture thinking is in place, it's time to determine your annual marketing budget.

For entrepreneurs and small business owners, allocating a marketing budget is always a difficult task because unlike a more established brand with existing revenue and past learning, a younger business doesn't have success analysis to draw from.

A common rule of thumb for business-to-business, (B2B) companies is the marketing budget should be a percentage of gross revenue, around 2-5% allocated to marketing your products and services annually. For business-to-consumer (B2C) companies, the proportion is generally higher, between 5-10%.

Marketing budget is required to scale your business, otherwise it will be difficult to get the traction you are looking for. And a bigger budget doesn't necessarily guarantee your success. It's important to set an annual marketing budget that aligns with your business goals with a plan to turn prospects into customers.

Take your annual budget and create categories based on key deliverables within the strategy, then slice it over 12-months, giving you a monthly view of spend by category. Build the marketing budget with these key categories in mind:

**Staff** – Account for staffing resources you might need. You could add full-time staff and freelancers as two budget lines depending on your needs, set an amount for one or both. The costs associated with onboarding full-time employees should also be included here.

**Software** – Every business requires software to meet core marketing needs. From CRM platforms for customer marketing, to social media management and analytical tools to track and measure your success.

**Advertising** – This category can have sub-items beneath such as print ads, native ads, search engine ads, and social media promotions. Think about whether you need outside support to create the advertising in these areas and budget accordingly.

**Content Creation** – We talk a lot about content through-out the book, and good content creation requires focus and budget to be done well. Content is the key to a well-crafted sales funnel, and warrants having it as its own budget category.

**Sponsorship/Events** – Depending on your strategy, you may need to allocate budget to partnership opportunities or for conducting virtual or life events. This might include supporting a local chamber of commerce event or hosting a webinar with outside speakers.

**Media** – It's best to set-up a media budget category as this accounts for the spend to reach your audience online and through print media. Here you can add lines for any social media sites and search engine marketing activities your plan calls for. The tactics you determine as part of your marketing plan will factor into how much you budget to allocate.

Once you have set your marketing budget for the year, it's important to review it monthly and update it against your actual spend. This is also an effective way to monitor your monthly invoices against your allotted budget.

**Budgeting** - When determining how much to invest in building and filling your sales funnel consider the maximum amount you would spend to close a sale. Include the volume and sales revenue you will need to grow your business. From there you can work back to determine an acceptable budget to achieve your sales targets. Investigate industry standard conversion if you haven't already bench marked expected conversion rates. Consider the long-term investment, with the building of the brand, good will, and a prospect database, don't limit spend to only immediate sales conversions.

Now with a Marketing Strategy in place, it's time to develop and launch your marketing plan.

# Develop an Integrated Marketing Plan

## Building the Foundation for Business Growth

To attract your buyers there are more online and offline marketing channels today than ever before. Your buyers are inundated with communications across diverse and widespread media. It's becoming increasingly more challenging to determine where to spend your marketing dollars to grow your business. Can an integrated marketing plan really help grow your business?

Company's today with an integrated marketing communication plan are better prepared to excel in today's market. When you plan wisely, you can get your message heard above all the noise and reach the buyers you're seeking. We'll explain the critical importance of having a plan, what goes into one and the success other businesses have achieved in filling the sales funnel.

## 5 Ways an Integrated Marketing Communication Drives Better and More Sales

To keep up with opportunities, your marketing plan needs to include a multi-channel and multi-media approach. Whether the marketing team is large or small, or divided by segments, products, or channels, it is essential to roll out an integrated marketing communications plan to maintain a consistent brand message across every touch point, and deliver a consistent and positive, omni-channel experience. Whether you are marketing to businesses or consumers, you'll reap the following benefits with an integrated marketing communications plan.

### 1. **Builds Credibility**

Your brand becomes more credible when you share one message across all channels. If you have a different brand message on every channel, your buyers will receive mixed messages about your services, which reduces purchases and your brand's credibility. Recent research by the Canadian Marketing Association (CMA) [ii] found that maintaining a consistent message can improve brand perception by nearly 70%.

## 2. Increases Recall and Purchases

The more you repeat your message across channels, the more likely your clients will remember it. The CMA found that integrated campaigns are 31% more effective at building brands. Another interesting recall concept is the mere exposure effect, where repetition increases liking. In fact, having one constant message across multiple channels can improve purchase intent by as much as 90%.

## 3. Reaches Your Audience

45% of companies now use more channels to research products or services, 70% of consumers use three channels [iii] or more and 88 percent of consumers pre-research their buys online before making a purchase either online or in-store. If you want to drive your buyers to making a purchase, using multiple channels is important to reinforce your message on every channel they visit.

## 4. Improves Clarity

Your buyers care about the value you can provide, so it's essential to ensure that, regardless of the channel they use, they clearly understand your value proposition. Clarity becomes even more critical as more companies adopt group decision-making processes. In 2023, an average of six to ten people were involved in purchasing decisions for complex sales, according to Gartner, a global research organization. When these decision-makers reconvene to discuss their findings, it is crucial that they all have a consistent understanding of your company and its message.

## 5. Reduces Your Cost to Acquire Customers

Having integrated marketing communications allows your marketing campaigns to become more effective. With one message consistently sent out to buyers, you can reinforce your competitive position using fewer channels. Also, if you center content around one message, you can modify it for each channel you use, lessening your content creation cost. Reducing your acquisition costs means, you can capture more sales without increasing your marketing spend.

How an Integrated Marketing Communications Plan Makes Your Marketing More Effective and Cost-Efficient

To ensure your marketing efforts are both effective and cost-efficient, begin by defining clear objectives within an integrated marketing plan. Align these objectives with your overall business goals and outline the expected outcomes. This approach keeps your marketing team unified and focused on achieving the same targets while optimizing resources. An integrated plan not only serves as a strategic roadmap but also provides a framework for monitoring progress and making necessary adjustments. As you develop your plan, consider the following:

**Target Audience**

Understanding your buyers' industries can help you tailor your message while showcasing your subject matter expertise, which was found to be important for 64% of B2B buyers. In general, consider who you want to target and what their preferred research channels are. As a result, you will be able to reach them more effectively.

**Budget**

Every channel has a different cost, whether it is measured by Cost Per Click (CPC) when launching PPC social media or search engine marketing campaigns or by impressions or reach across online and offline media. Your budget will directly impact the number of channels you can invest in, your offer, the presentation of your message and how well you can manage and track your performance.

## Competition

Buyers will only choose your product or service if you are offering something valued that is perceived as superior to the competition. So, identifying your competitors' offerings and their message to buyers will help you determine how to set yourself apart. Also, if your competitors are dominant in one of the main channels, then your plan may be to find some unoccupied space that you can succeed in.

## Channels

With so many marketing channels you can't dominate the airways across all of them.  Knowing your audience, choose the channels you can cost-effectively reach with your buyers.  Make sure you include channels that align with your buyer's journey and your sales funnels if your goal is to drive more sales.  Whether it is a social media platform, search engines, print, events, radio, or email, invest wisely – don't overextend your budget.  Check out what your competition is doing within the same channels to see if you can outbid them.  And remember, you need to drive frequency within and across channels to get your buyers to notice and respond to your message.

## Communication Types

Across channels, you need to provide consistency, but how you package the message, needs to be in sync with the channel you are using.  If it's YouTube, you'll need to package your message in a video, if it's a blog, it's text, images, and infographics.  If it's a presentation your message will be in PowerPoint.  To ensure it is impactful and rememberable, how you deliver your message is just as important.

**Unique Value Proposition**

Once you have determined who you are targeting, your conveyed value proposition should be aligned with their needs. Ensure that your message is powerful, clear, and concise so that it will attract buyers.

## 5 Marketing Tactics

In reviewing your overall marketing strategy, focus on certain marketing tactics as a part of the plan. Listing four to five main tactical initiatives will help your organization work towards a plan. Also refer to the section *Use Channels more Likely to Convert* to help build out your marketing plan. Remember to keep your plans flexible and agile so you can take advantage of opportunities as they arise.

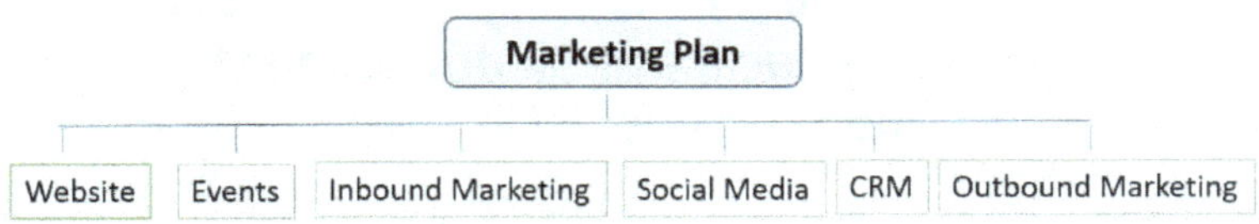


## Role of the Website

Determine whether you need to revamp or build a new website. Address why your website is so important and the role it plays in attracting, engaging, and converting your personas into buyers. Additional content and resources for your website plans will be listed here. Include how to measure efforts and what success will look like. Consider the number of new web site visitors, bounce rates, time on page, visitors converted into sales, event conversion rate, number of leads acquired, event registrations, newsletter sign-ups, etc.

## Email Marketing & Events Strategy

Understand the role that events, and email marketing will play. Explain the strategy and goals for each. Also address promotions, segmentation and how other channels will be integrated.

## Inbound Marketing

Determine the mix of inbound marketing tactics needed to pull-in your buyers. It may include SEO, a content strategy and a PPC campaign. Some of the inbound marketing tactics are further explained below and in other sections.

## Search Engine Optimization (SEO) Efforts

Outline the SEO strategy and its importance in achieving the overall goals. Explain how it will be incorporated throughout your website, social media, and content marketing efforts.

## Content Marketing

Content plays a crucial role in your marketing plan and in building your brand and selling your products and services. Explain how it will be used, who will be creating it and why it will improve search and attract buyers. Discuss any changes from the previous year, list KPIs, explain how content will be distributed and outline rough goals for the plan. And include additional resources needed.

## Social Media Marketing

Determine which social media channels are important for reaching your target audience.  Include strategies on how to keep a consistent presence, build relationships, gain followers, get likes, etc. Also, determine the goals for each social media account, and how to maintain brand consistency across all channels. Address the role social will play in distributing content and bringing members and potential buyers back to the website, signing up for events, renewing subscriptions, purchasing products or services, etc.

### CRM

With CRM (Customer Relationship Management), identify the goals, whether to reduce attrition, increase share of wallet or raise your net promoter score. Include strategies that will meet these goals.

### Outbound Marketing

Outbound marketing refers to outgoing campaigns to pull-in the buyer. They may include email campaigns, SMS, social selling, and telemarketing. Define the role and goals you expect to achieve by adding them to the marketing plan.

## Successfully Execute an Integrated Marketing Plan

Once you plan your work, it's time to work your plan! Here are 5 key components of a successful plan:

Consumers spend more than a quarter of the day engaging with digital content. When making buying decisions the average customer engages with 3-5 pieces of content before talking to a sales rep.[iv] If your goal is to grow your business, it's important you're writing great content that is delivering your brand message consistently and tailored to your audience.

With your digital sales funnel, the content needs to hold the audience's attention – be relevant, meaningful, and persuasive in driving the behaviour you're seeking at each stage in the buyers' journey. If the goal is to drive demand and capture leads, the content needs have enough value for them to be willing to exchange their contact information.

With so many online properties and platforms, you need to be selective based on your target audience preferences. You don't need to be everywhere, just where your buyers are. Finally, make sure you're leveraging online data to personalize your marketing campaigns because personalization can increase sales by 19%.[v]

Offline

Even with the increase in available online channels, offline marketing remains important. Offline marketing, like direct mail, print ads, demonstrations and events can effectively fill your sales pipeline. Being more tactile and interactive, some buyers may prefer offline channels. Both B2B and B2C have become highly creative with experimental marketing tactics, making this an important part of their marketing strategy.

## Customize Content

Although it's important to have a consistent brand message, you'll need to make sure your content is adapted or developed based on the channel your buyers are engaging in. Invest only where your customers congregate and balance your efforts with compelling formats, integration, and personalization. A winning campaign has enough familiarity to tie campaign elements together but enough novelty to engage with complementary content. [vi]

## Customer Experience

Your message won't be well-received unless it's delivered within a positive customer experience. Good customer experience is when you meet or exceed the expectations of your customers, clients, and prospects at each touchpoint down the sales funnel. Every communication – every touchpoint, online and offline can impact your ability to grow your business.  A positive experience builds loyalty, referrals, and more sales.



Businesses that excel know the value of data. Gathering data along the way will go far in growing your business.  Without continuously improving, you can't successfully grow your business – if you don't measure you can't improve. Gathering rich data on your customers will help you serve up the right content at the right time across the right channel. That's the key ingredient in a successful integrated marketing plan.


# Reap the Benefits of a Thought Leadership Strategy


A thought leadership strategy focuses less on content that sells and more on content that establishes you as an expert in your field. This type of strategy fills your sales funnel by earning you credibility and rapport. When you freely provide accurate information and consistent advice, buyers reciprocate by purchasing your products and services and encouraging their colleagues to buy from you.

This strategy can be effective in moving sales opportunities down funnel including when you have many stakeholders influencing the buying decision. When you address the concerns of a purchasing agent right up to the c-suite level you are guaranteed to win more RFPs (request for proposals). Less price-sensitive buyers and longer-term client relationships are additional benefits for launching a thought leadership content strategy.

Growing in Popularity and Importance.

More companies are adopting a thought leadership strategy and creating more meaningful content. In a survey [vii] of more than 1,300 business decision-makers by Edelman and LinkedIn found that 91 percent of business decision-makers, and 73 percent of C-suite executives, considered thought leadership either important or critical to business growth. Nearly 40 percent of those surveyed, spent one to three hours a week reading this type of content.

A well-planned thought leadership strategy can differentiate your brand in a crowded marketplace and shift purchasing behaviour towards your product or service. When content gets shared, becomes searchable, and is well received among your target audience without needing a media budget, it could be considered one of the best marketing investments a growth-driven organization can make.

## How to Build Thought Leadership

If you are ready to embark on a thought leadership strategy, here are some of the key elements to position yourself as a leader and to start filling your sales funnel.

Anticipate and answer the questions your target audience and personas are seeking to have answered.

Select content that showcases other experts in the company, their expertise, knowledge, and opinion on a variety of topics that relate back to your product and service offering.

Use an authoritative voice in the google sphere and in every-day business dealings.

Make the content accessible. You need to make it available where your target audience resides. This can include your website and social media channels or through push out campaigns, like emails and webinars.

Follow SEO and social media rules.  Keywords play an important role, knowing the common terms your buyer uses to search for answers as well as hashtags makes it easier for your audience to discover your content.

Choose formats based on your audience preferences. Do they prefer videos over blogs?  Are they seeking answers more through whitepapers or podcasts?

Leverage influencers. Almost every industry has social media influencers as well as activists, bloggers, published authors and journalists.

What Type of Content Goes into a Thought Leadership Positioning Strategy?

Creating content doesn't have to be difficult, but it does require planning and thought. The question is whether you need outside help to get the content written or do you have great resources internally who are itching to show off their creative side and share their expertise? Either way, you only need a few key pieces of content to get you started and get your potential buyers engaged. Focus on the following:

**Blog post** – write an original blog post on a relevant topic – one that ties into your business offering, and offers value, and is informative. One blog a month is the minimum requirement to begin building your brand's reputation, but if you have writing support you should aim for two ore more. Post the blog to your website in the blog/insights section. Also, consider converting the blog into an article and loading it on LinkedIn, if that is where your target audience resides. The main difference between a blog versus an article is an article is typically longer in length than a blog (1500-5000 words) and may include interview style quotes from internal and external experts.

**Social media posts** – social media channels like LinkedIn, Facebook, Twitter, and Instagram are an important part of a marketing strategy and are the best place for you to promote the blog you've written. You can entice your business followers to read your blog by posting a short excerpt of the blog and include the link back to the blog on your website. It's important to drive potential customers to your site to read the blog. They will be more inclined to peruse the site's offerings. A content calendar is a great way to keep track of these and other business-related posts. Aim to post content 2-3 times a week to start and gauge interest and engagements over time. Adjust the posting schedule based on promotional needs.

**Research material** – original research and data are considered gold when it comes to thought leadership. When you speak authoritatively with research and statistics to back up opinions it strengthens the message exponentially. Plus, it makes great material to post on your social channels. And, if done right, you can create a great PR campaign with opportunities for the content to go viral and get seen.

**Webinars** – hold a webinar once you have great research material. By hosting a webinar, it provides the business with another sales opportunity to connect with its customers and give insights and value in an interactive setting.

**Videos** – today's social sphere is a prime spot for video content. Videos don't have to be long; they can be fun and engaging. Creating short videos with employees, owners and leaders often provides a glimpse of who the company is and what they stand for.

These are just a few easy tactics to incorporate into your thought leadership strategy and overall marketing plan. Just remember, it's not the quantity of content that matters, but the quality and relevance. Take the time to do an audit of your space and check-out the competition. And, remember content creation and thought leadership is one pillar of a growth plan, but most effective over the long-term. Be sure to give it the proper attention when developing your marketing plan.

# Have a Business Case for Your Marketing Plan

Some of the simplest sayings are the most accurate and this one is bang on when it comes to improving your financial performance. *"What doesn't get measured, doesn't get improved upon".*  It you don't look at the measurement of your efforts, with dedicated resources, you'll never know what's working and therefore, can't implement change or improvements. Measurement is the key to success. With every goal, a key performance indicator (KPI) should be assigned, reviewed, and repeated as it becomes a continuous test and learn loop. The following section will provide current thinking about marketing investment, and measurement that go into a business case. Whether it's campaign results, brand share of voice, or marketing ROI, measurement is the cornerstone of any successful growth driven organization.

## Measure Your Success

Marketing is changing rapidly, so it's important to monitor your success. The companies and customers you're targeting will face new challenges and may prefer new channels to obtain information. You need to be aware of these changes and decide whether you need to modify or keep your initial strategy in place. Also, you need to decide on what KPIs you want to observe, such as, sales data, number of new leads, and the channels bringing them in.

The KPIs used and what success ultimately looks like should tie back to the business objectives and marketing goals.

## How to Quantify Potential Sales Revenue from Marketing Opportunities

It is important in the planning stage to quantify potential sales revenue through assessing the marketing opportunities across key verticals, segments, affiliates, and sponsors. As a result of having a strong business case for your marketing plan, it will assist in prioritizing efforts and marketing investments.

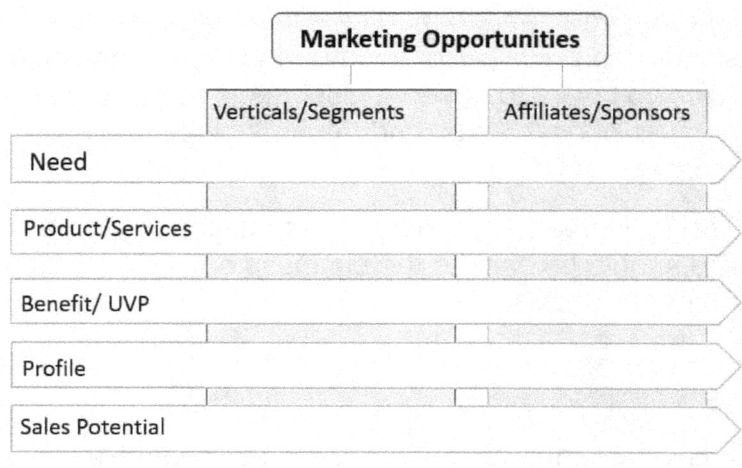


Case Studies: Starbucks, McDonalds, Dove

# CASE STUDIES: STARBUCKS, MCDONALDS, DOVE, OUTREACH.IO

## Starbucks – Expanding Global Presence through Strategic Planning

**Background:** Starbucks, a global coffeehouse chain, was facing the challenge of maintaining its growth trajectory while expanding into new international markets. The company needed to develop a strategic plan that would not only allow it to enter new markets effectively but also adapt to the diverse preferences and cultural differences of consumers around the world.

**Strategy:** Starbucks employed a comprehensive strategic planning process to guide its expansion efforts. This plan involved analyzing consumer trends and adapting their product offerings to fit the needs of different regions. For instance, Starbucks introduced menu items tailored to local tastes and preferences in various countries. Additionally, they focused on creating a consistent brand experience globally, while also allowing for localized marketing strategies that resonated with local cultures.

**Results:** The strategic plan was highly successful, allowing Starbucks to expand its global footprint significantly. By 2020, Starbucks had over 30,000 stores worldwide, with a strong presence in both established and emerging markets. The company's ability to adapt its products and marketing strategies to local preferences while maintaining a strong global brand identity was key to its success.

**Key Takeaways:** This case study demonstrates the importance of strategic planning in successfully expanding a business into new markets. By carefully analyzing consumer behavior and local market conditions, Starbucks was able to grow its business while maintaining its brand integrity. Strategic planning enabled Starbucks to achieve sustainable growth and become one of the most recognized brands globally.

## McDonald's – Adapting to Local Markets

**Background:** McDonald's, the world's largest fast-food chain, has succeeded in large part due to its ability to adapt its menu and marketing strategies to local tastes and cultures in different regions of the world.

**Strategy:** McDonald's uses a "glocal" strategy—think globally, act locally. For instance, in India, where a significant portion of the population is vegetarian, McDonald's introduced the McAloo Tikki, a potato-based burger, and offers a menu without beef or pork. In Japan, McDonald's has introduced products like the Teriyaki Burger to cater to local tastes. The company also tailors its marketing campaigns to resonate with local cultures and traditions, ensuring relevance in each market.

**Results:** This strategy has allowed McDonald's to maintain its status as a global leader in the fast-food industry. By respecting local customs and preferences, McDonald's has been able to attract a diverse customer base and establish a strong presence in markets around the world.

**Key Takeaways:** McDonald's success demonstrates the importance of cultural sensitivity and market adaptation in global marketing. By understanding and catering to local tastes and preferences, McDonald's has been able to build a brand that resonates with consumers across different regions.

## Dove – The Campaign for Real Beauty

**Background:** Dove, a personal care brand, launched the "Campaign for Real Beauty" in 2004 to address the narrow definitions of beauty perpetuated by the media. The campaign aimed to celebrate the natural beauty of all women, regardless of shape, size, or age.

**Strategy:** Dove's strategy was to challenge the traditional beauty standards set by the industry. They used real women, not models, in their advertisements to convey that beauty comes in all forms. The campaign included TV commercials, print ads, and a series of viral videos, including the famous "Dove Evolution" video, which showcased the extensive retouching that goes into creating a "perfect" model.

**Results:** The "Campaign for Real Beauty" was a massive success. It sparked global conversations about beauty standards and body positivity, leading to a significant increase in brand recognition and consumer loyalty. Dove's sales increased from $2.5 billion to over $4 billion in the campaign's first ten years.

**Key Takeaways:** Dove's campaign is a prime example of how a brand can differentiate itself by challenging industry norms and connecting with consumers on a deeper, more meaningful level. By promoting authenticity and inclusivity, Dove was able to build a strong, loyal customer base and significantly boost its brand equity.

## Outreach.io – From Startup to a $1.1 Billion SaaS Company

**Background:** Outreach.io, a SaaS company providing sales engagement software, started as a small startup facing stiff competition in the SaaS space. To achieve rapid growth and establish a strong market position, the company needed a strategic approach that would enable them to scale quickly while ensuring their marketing efforts were cost-effective.

**Strategy:** Outreach.io focused on a data-driven approach to their marketing strategy. They meticulously tracked key performance indicators (KPIs) to inform their decisions and optimize their marketing campaigns. The company also invested in strategic acquisitions to expand their product offerings and market reach. By aligning their marketing and sales teams, Outreach.io ensured that every marketing initiative was targeted, measurable, and aligned with the company's overall growth objectives.

**Results:** This strategy paid off handsomely. Outreach.io grew from a small startup to a $1.1 billion SaaS giant in a relatively short period. Their focus on data-driven decision-making and strategic growth allowed them to scale efficiently, maximize their marketing ROI, and achieve significant market penetration.

**Key Takeaways:** This case study underscores the importance of a data-driven marketing strategy in achieving rapid growth. By focusing on measurable outcomes and aligning marketing efforts with broader business objectives, Outreach.io was able to scale its operations and become a dominant player in the

SaaS market. This example highlights the value of strategic planning and goal setting in ensuring that marketing efforts are both effective and cost-efficient.

## JUMPin2it Resources: Your Path to Success

At JUMPin2it, we empower business owners with the tools and inspiration they need to succeed. Explore our resource library, podcasts, networking events, consulting, and training to ignite your growth and drive your business forward. Ready to take the leap? Dive into all that JUMPin2it has to offer.

Visit: https://360integralmarketing.com/jump-in-2-it/

# JUMPin2it SECTION II - BREAKTHRU MARKETING PLANS AND TACTICS

"Many of life's failures are people who did not realize how close they were to success when they gave up."
– Thomas Edison

Whether building a brand, growing sales, or retaining existing customer relationships, the way to get there involves a bit of science, art, and a whole lot of hard work, patience, and good judgement. The following section provides more ways to be effective and efficient with your marketing. We provide a myriad of sales funnel techniques, strategies, tactics, and tools, to optimize results and grow the sales faster and better.

Grab your pen and paper (or your laptop) and get ready to work. We believe that success is based on 20% skill /effort and 80% is in the strategy!  The information you uncover over the next few pages will form the foundation of your marketing plan. Here's your chance to define each one and dare to be exceed expectations.

# 11 Ways to Persuade Your Buyers

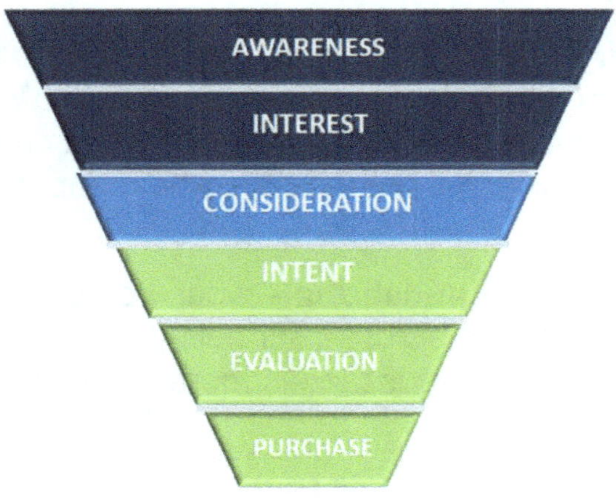


With solid strategies and a plan in place you can't stop there!  Time to transcend all your knowledge, research, insights, and resources into sales funnels and persuasion sequences that drive up repeatable sales and a scalable business.

Before you build your sales funnel, consider these key marketing drivers and the importance they play in filling your sales funnel. The better you get at developing, harnessing, and implementing them, the more successful you'll be at capturing opportunities and converting them into sales.

**Brand Story** – any good brand has a story and can articulate what they stand for in a few words. With developing your brand strategy, be sure you can communicate your vision, mission, and company values.

**Integrated Communications** – when you deliver a consistent message across channels you build trust and credibility. Your message is more easily heard and remembered.

**Marketing Tactics** – not all tactics are created equal, choose tactics that will drive the outcome you're looking for. Based on the different stages of the buying journey some tactics will be more effective and less costly than others. Marketing tactics will be covered in more detail as you read on.

**Content** – content creation is the new normal. An integrated content strategy is necessary to tell your story and showcase what you have to offer. Good content will increase visitor traffic to your website and accelerate the volume of buyers down the sales funnel. Find a content niche that differentiates your business from the competition and helps you stand out from the crowd.

**Thought Leadership** – is there a difference between creating content and being a thought leader? The answer is YES! Thought leadership is about showcasing your knowledge on a topic and having data to support it. A great way to be a thought leader is to publish insights on a segment of the population that consumers or industry stakeholders are interested in and include it in your content plan.

**Segmentation and Personas** – understand your audience. With the work you completed on your target audience and personas will help make your content more relevant and provide best ways to reach them.

**Personalization** – personalizing your communications increases engagement and improves sales conversion rates. Plan to use technology to create high tech, high touch marketing and sales communications.

**Technology** – as mentioned when building your strategy, technology can play a critical part in persuading your buyers to act. CRM tools like HubSpot, SalesForce, Zoho capture customer information that enables greater personalization and real-time responsiveness to client inquiries. Online chats capture buyers when they are on your site, manage queries and provide answers to questions. Website tracking of visitors and other metrics such as traffic source, visitor profile, engagement activity and their performance are important in determining the success of the sales funnel.

**Channels** – being an integral part of any marketing plan is determining the channels to invest in to reach your buyers. Selecting the most effective channels can reduce your marketing costs and potentially your timelines to close.

**Persuasion Sequence** – whether you're looking to attract new customers from industry conferences, digital strategies (paid leads/Google AdWords), customer referrals or through social media channels, there must be a mix of these and other tactics to be most effective.

**Partnerships** – affiliates, brokers, influencers, and partnerships can play an important role in acquiring new customers. Combining marketing efforts with a non-competitor going after the same target audience, can reduce your marketing costs and remove barriers to reaching your buyers.  A well-respected partner can open doors, build immediate trust, generate referrals, and give you access to their customer base to generate sales.

Be prepared to phase-in your plan, continuously test, and adjust based on the opportunities. However, omitting or under utilizing any of these key marketing building blocks can impact your ability to grow a successful business and your customer base.


## Your Sales Loop to Get and Grow Customers



The sales funnel is often shown as an inverted triangle. However, it's not always the case. The buyer may jump from the top to the bottom and up to the middle of the sales funnel. Marketing can influence but not command how the buyer will behave.  Below is another way of looking at your sales funnel, from getting the customer to growing customer sales.

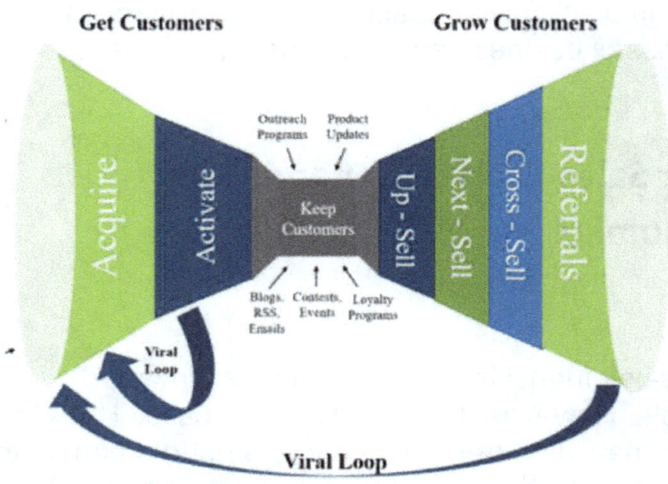


## Develop a Series of Repeatable Steps

Building a sales funnel is an iterative process. You can refer to past successes and research, but the results lie with the actions your buyers take in the market and how effective you are at filling your sales funnel and converting those opportunities into sales.

As more sales are initiated by your buyers going online, the game never stands still. Buyers have become savvier and technology, media outlets, artificial intelligence, accessibility to data, competitive landscape and government policies keep evolving and changing. You can't rely on past successes to propel your business forward. Your sales funnel requires constant maintenance and upkeep. Business owners and marketers who've been successful in growing sales funnels, follow a series of continuous steps for locating and converting potential buyers into profitable customers, and then looping them back into acquiring more products, services and referrals.

To help reduce the complexity of what goes into creating your sales loop, we simplified the steps as follows:

**Find:** discover new clients and sales opportunities with current clients using analytics, online footprint tracking and past successes.

**Nurture**: provide relevant and targeted content to your potential and current customers to encourage them to engage with your brand.

**Convert:** win over your buyers by generating rewarding interactions that are financially profitable for your business.

## Invest in Growing Your Customer Relationships

You may already feel your business is doing everything it can to acquire new customers. But what plans have you put in place to retain existing customers, and how are you interacting and communicating with your current client base? After all, it's common knowledge that it's far easier and less costly to keep an existing customer than to onboard a new one.

When your customers feel that you value their business, loyalty, brand preference and sales tend to grow. And when they benefit from valuable advice, focused support, and uninterrupted service, they could very well talk about their fantastic customer experience to all their friends and colleagues. And that could mean more referral business for you. Remember, the loyal and well-serviced customer can become your best brand ambassador. And that kind of marketing doesn't cost a penny.

Five Ways to Maintain and Improve Your Customer Relationships

Tap into the opportunities to grow your business with your current customers. Here are some tips on how to achieve this:

Deliver relevant, timely content that solves customers' immediate and long-term challenges:

- Make it easy for customers to connect with you
- Put an inbound 1-800 customer service number in place
- Set up virtual meetings with an online scheduling app
- Prioritize online chatting with customers
- Develop easy, time-saving online FAQs for customers
- Deepen the customer relationship by offering more products and services
- Engage in your customers' channel of preference (if they are reaching out through social media respond to them through social media if their channel preference is email, respect and use that channel)
- Be responsive to all customers, regardless of the channel they choose (because they need to feel valued and trust you to deliver on your promise)

How you maintain and grow your business is by staying focused. Identify and eliminate, unnecessary expenses, outsource non-core competencies and use the extra money to invest in your business and effective marketing efforts that deliver measurable results.

## Be Where Your Buyers Are – Online

If your sales previously relied on bricks and mortar stores, face-to-face meetings, tradeshows, or events, it's time to re-evaluate your marketing strategy.

With the COVID-19 pandemic leading to city lockdowns and widespread isolation, the internet has become a vital resource for people seeking connection, information, and improvement in their personal and professional lives. For businesses, this presents a crucial opportunity to elevate their digital communication strategies. By having a well-crafted digital marketing strategy in place, your business can effectively engage with your audience while ensuring that every marketing dollar is spent wisely and efficiently, maximizing both impact and cost-efficiency.

Important Questions to Ask When it Comes to Reaching Your Buyers Online

- Does your business have a reputable online presence and an intuitive and easy-to-use online interface?
- Have you implemented a Pay per Click (PPC) online advertising campaign to pull in buyers searching for your services?
- Do you have a social media campaign that engages with your potential customers?
- Is your website and content optimized for search engines when clients are browsing and researching online?
- Is your website delivering a superior user experience – is it easy to navigate, and explain your value proposition and how to buy your products and services?

If you have not invested in an omnichannel digital marketing strategy, with consistently aligned messaging and customer experiences across channels and platforms, it's not too late to start. If you are already invested in online, consider devoting even more resources to this critically important area.

## Six Ways to Sell More Effectively in the Digital World

With social distancing becoming the preventative measure to contain a crisis, investing or reallocating resources to different sales channels may be the opportunity you have overlooked, until now. Here are six ideas to help you sell more effectively in the digital world:

- Build eCommerce functionality on your site so customers can order your goods and services directly
- Make sure you offer quick, inexpensive delivery to online shoppers' home and business
- Add functionality to your website so users can easily book virtual appointments
- Offer webinars in place of face-to-face presentations
- Implement an online chat tool so online buyers and browsers have a way to get their questions quickly answered
- Post a comprehensive online FAQ on your site, with strong search functionality

If you are selling knowledge and expertise, take the time to build compelling online content that provides prospects with valuable information on how to solve their most pressing problems. Make that content available across online channels and throughout the digital ecosystem. This is your chance to build your brand, strengthen relationships, create trust, and grow demand for your services.

Resources
Government of Canada Public Health up to date news on the Coronavirus

CNBC how to protect your business in midst of a coronavirus outbreak

With marketing technology today, the task of executing a successful strategy and gathering a 360 view of your buyers for tracking and optimizing efforts is more within reach today than it's ever been.

# Marketing Automation and Artificial Intelligence (AI)

All businesses and industries of various sizes are starting to adopt marketing automation and artificial Intelligence to streamline and improve their go-to-market efforts. On average, 51% of companies are currently using marketing automation. With more than half of B2B companies (58%) plan to adopt technology according to Ultimate Marketing Automation stats. [viii]

8 Benefits of Marketing Automation

- Automates the buying process
- Segments and profiles your buyers
- Integrates with sales and marketing
- Improves relationships with buyers
- Gives markers a 360 view of their buyers
- Generates more sales-ready leads

- Increases sales productivity
- Makes marketing more strategic

## Automates the Buying Process

Some of the benefits of AI and marketing automation is it provides Marketing and Sales with a new set of tools to accelerate past the lack of face-to-face connections in cyberspace. Today's methods guide prospects through the buying process while delivering timely, engaging content and gathering key buying indicators.

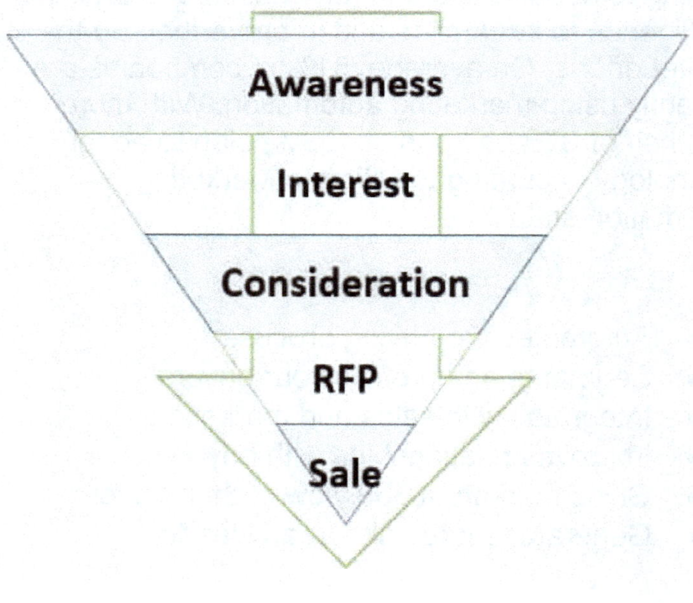

## Segments and Profiles Your Buyers

Contacts can be segmented based on their buying cycle, needs, geographies or any meaningful way you need to segment them. Furthermore, segmentation is not limited to demographics or firmographics but includes many channels including social media, email, and web pages.  As a result of the platform gathering attributes and profile data across channels – marketers can segment lists and follow through the next best action.

## Integrates Sales with Marketing

Automated marketing uses the information gathered from digital body language to gauge interest and intent when it comes to your brand. It's the modern and efficient way to target your efforts so they work best. Information gathered, either through forms, online activity or social media, data can be pushed through a sales force automation (SFA) system or a CRM system for sales follow-up and conversion tracking.

## Improves Relationships with Buyers

Personalized content is key. Buyers want unique, targeted content at each stage of their research. Marketing automation simplifies the process of getting the right content to the right buyer at the right time. With real-time personalization and customization of content across channels, you can better deepen relationships. Because you can optimize a content strategy through a/b testing, engagement can continuously be improved. All this translates to having more interested and informed buyers about your brand, services, and products. As a result, each engagement gives Marketing the opportunity to deliver more sales-ready leads.

### Gives Marketing a 360 View of Their Buyers

The marketing automation tool can track engagement across channels and links it back to the customer's profile. Metrics can include but not limited to website visits, email return visitors across product pages, shares on social media, video views, email opens, click-through rates, and form submissions. This wealth of data enables you to have a 360 view of your buyer. With this business intelligence, you can measure the quality of the lead, track the impact of each touchpoint, generate an attribution model and measure MROI (Marketing Return on Investment).

### Generates More Sales-Ready Leads

As every touchpoint can be tracked, including website visits, downloads, and social media activity, it enables the platform to perform automatic scoring to qualify, and prioritize the leads for sales follow-up or to generate another communication to follow warm the lead. Some marketing automated campaigns can include the following:

- Trigger-based marketing messages
- Infrequent "drip-feed" emails to maintain interest
- Personalized emails

## Increases Sales Productivity

Marketing automation drives a 14.5% increase in sales productivity according to Nucleus Research.[ix]  Sales receiving more sales-ready leads reduces their sales cycle-time and cold calling efforts. It also, streamlines tasks for entering contacts into a marketing program, accessing marketing tools, and using email templates. Furthermore, having insight into their buyers' interests, including the frequency and recency of the content they view can steer the salesperson into having the right conversations with their buyers.

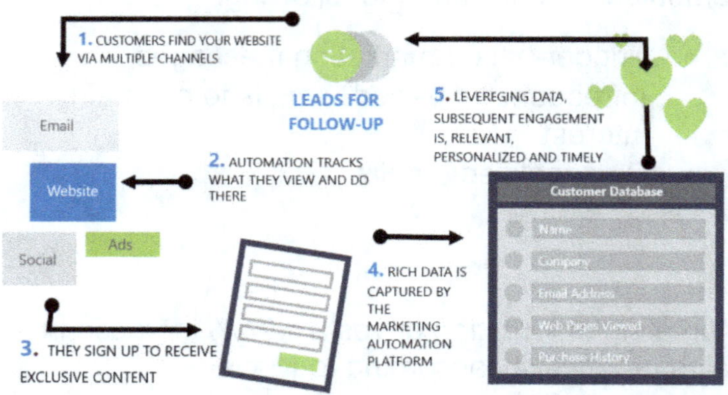


## Makes Marketing More Strategic

Marketing automation reduces 12.2% in marketing overhead overall. Many steps are now streamlined, automated, and measured. And, when you eliminate manual tasks, it allows your marketing team to focus on being more strategic. With the incredible wealth of business intelligence captured through marketing automation and the integration of CRM, Marketing becomes a more strategic partner in improving business performance.

# Don't Waste Money on the Wrong Marketing Technology

## Choosing the Best MarTech Stack Is About Improving Your Marketing Efforts

What Is a MarTech stack? MarTech stands for Marketing Technology. It defines the software or marketing platforms marketing teams use to plan, execute, manage, and measure marketing initiatives. A MarTech stack represents the whole suite of marketing tools an organization would use across their marketing programs.

## The Value of MarTech

Marketing professionals are scrambling to find the best ways to identify and engage with their customers. As a result, knowing how to select the best MarTech stack for your business has become an important part of executing your strategy.

What has changed for marketers in the last few years is the ability to integrate systems together so that no matter what channel your audience is on, you can track and deepen the engagement in meaningful ways. The best part is tracking is now available across channels, making insights remarkable.

Proving a MROI (marketing return on investment) has become easier.

The automation component easily allows for personalization and segmented communication without adding to staff time or increasing staff size. As a result, you can provide meaningful communications to your audience, using triggers that your audience initiates themselves, so they get to decide what and when they want it, without any staff involvement.

Because of multiple campaigns and multiple strategies, there are some limitations to integrating systems. To minimize costs, reduce efforts and drive better performance, digital marketing has become a blending of technology with marketing know-how. Therefore, choosing the best MarTech stack becomes an integral part of a marketer's role.

## Different types of MarTech tools

MarTech stack helps manage the complexity of integrated digital marketing campaigns. The optimal MarTech stack ensures better campaign performance for your business.

With over 5,000 MarTech [x] options available, finding the right tools can be a daunting task. In helping select the best MarTech stack you will need for proper management and tracking of your campaigns, we have grouped them into three categories: management tools, tracking tools, and marketing campaign tools.

Below are types that fall into these three categories:

## Management Tools

CRM (Customer Relationship Management)

Data Management Platform

CMS (Content Management System)

Social Media Management

## Tracking Tools

Attribution Solution

Website Tracking

Programmatic Platform

Google Analytics

## Marketing Campaign Tools

Marketing Automation

Dynamic Ad Platform

Email Marketing

Event Marketing

CRO (Conversion Rate Optimization)

If you want to acquire new customers and generate repeat buys to grow your return on marketing investment (ROMI), you need to run campaigns on multiple platforms with multiple strategies. Without a MarTech stack, proper data management, and a team who understands how to get the best out of the technology, you will lose the game against the competition.

# How to Succeed with MarTech

## BUSINESS STRATEGY

Let your business strategy guide your choices. As with other investments, your MarTech tools should match-up with your business goals. A go-to-market plan will dictate the set of marketing tools to achieve those goals.

## ALIGN MARKETING WITH IT

In marketing you need to be armed with the data and intelligence; capturing, managing, analyzing and delivering data sets. IT also needs to understand the intelligence to make the entire business successful.

## BUILD FOR THE FUTURE

As you expand and scale your business you will need more sophisticated technical capabilities. Consider what tools you will require to support the business you're building, not just the one you're running today.

## MEASURE SUCCESS

Understand your customers, set short and long-term goals, and implement the technologies that will support your business objectives with them in mind. Key metrics should align with Marketing, IT and the organization's agenda.

# Develop and Refine Your Multi-Touch Persuasion Sequence

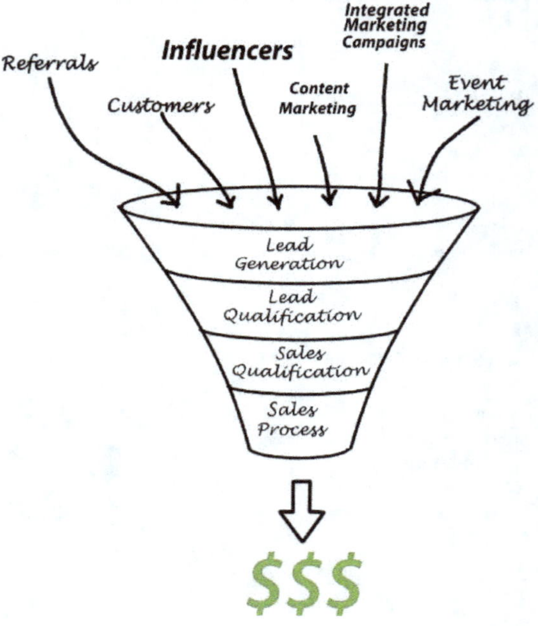



Building Your Persuasion Sequence

Digital sales funnels are online persuasion sequences that motivate buyers to make purchasing decisions. A digital sales funnel mapped out will help identify the opportunities, messaging and triggers that will move a prospect into a buyer.

Experts say it takes on average seven touchpoints before you can make a sale. The renowned marketer, Dr. Jeffrey Lant created the "Rule of Seven" where you must contact your buyers a minimum of seven times in an 18-month period for your potential buyers to remember you. Jay Abraham claims you need to contact someone seven times before they say "yes" to a sale.

With the need for multi-touches before prospects are willing to buy from you, thought leadership and demand generation content plays a vital role in creating a multi-touchpoint strategy to push buyers down the sales funnel. To measure their success, it's about measuring engagement each step of the way. When promoting your content across online channels, KPIs can include, whitepapers or case study downloads, webinar attendees, events registrations, social media engagement metrics, webpage visits to the attribution they made to create a sale.

## Building Your Persuasion Sequence

There are many ways you can build your persuasion sequence, using varies touch points and strategies to persuade your buyer. Below are 27 ways in total! It has been broken down into three steps as follows:

**Inbound** tactics to capture potential buyers, providing them with compelling reasons to visit your site, landing page or to reach out to call.

**Landing page** is your website page, or microsite where you guide them to take specific set of actions. It can be to purchase a product, convince them to register for an event or have them exchange their contact information for future follow-up.

**Off page** tactics can be treated as another stage in your persuasion sequence. It's a chance to follow-up with them after they complete or abandon a task and left your site or landing page. You can use this opportunity to drive them back to your landing page, upsell, cross-sell, convert them into a sales-ready lead or close a sale.

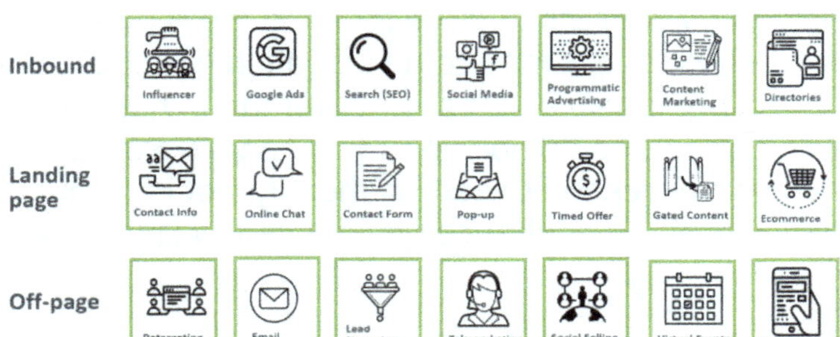



## Follow-Up with Visitors After They Leave Your Landing Page

About 95% of visitors on your landing page never turn into a sales opportunity. However, there's a few things you can do to bring them back into your persuasion sequence:

**Add an exit pop-up form**, remind them of the offer or another less committed offer such as signing up for a newsletter.

**Use remarketing ads** to follow your visitors across the online network and/or Facebook with a series of ads encouraging them to come back. (Check PPC Campaigns.)

89

**Follow-up with an email** using a marketing automation platform. If you've tied their IP address to their email address and are meeting the regulatory requirements for email communication, you can send them a personalized email or enter them into a lead nurturing or drip campaign. If you can personalize the communication based on the interest or pages they viewed, your chances for success will greatly increase.

*"Up to 95% of qualified prospects on your website are there to research and not yet ready to talk with sales, however, up to 70% will eventually buy from you – or your competitors." … Brian Carroll, author of Lead Generation for a Complex Sale.*

## Effective Outbound and Inbound Lead Generation Programs

When building your sales funnel, it's important to know the difference between inbound and outbound lead generation, and which is better to use for generating new cost-effective sales opportunities.  If you are an ecommerce or SaaS subscription business, especially targeting SME or B2C you will heavily rely on buyers finding you online and completing the transaction without them having to speak with a sales rep. If that's the case, you could probably skip this section.

Lead generation is when you pass a sales opportunity to a Sales Rep to close. Up to now most of tactics we discussed are inbound, whereas the clients are coming to you or what can also be referred to as a pull strategy. Outbound lead generation is a push strategy where you are actively contacting your potential buyers to generate sales opportunities.

**Inbound Lead Generation**

Inbound is about building it and they will come. It's always great when you only need to answer the phone to generate business.

Inbound requires an investment in building all your digital marketing assets, with engaging content to draw in your buyers; answering their questions and providing the solutions with a great user experience. Lead capture can be through gated content. They demonstrate their interest by completing a form in exchange for valued content or by scheduling an appointment, completing a contact us form, chatting online, calling or emailing.

**Pros**: If a prospect is requesting to be contacted, they are much easier to close, it's a shorter sales cycle and typically the buyer has done most of their homework and knows what they are looking for.

It tends to be a more positive experience, as the potential buyer has initiated the conversation. Works very well for higher volume or lower costs sales deals, whereas SME or consumers are more likely to complete a contact form or call than large enterprise sales opportunity.

**Cons**:  You can't easily control who will becoming to your site and requesting to be contacted. It takes time to manage the enquiries. You need resources committed to respond on a timely basis. Not responding quickly can dramatically reduce the chances the lead will convert and reflects poorly on the brand.  And, if you are using gated content to generate leads, you will need to filter through what is a sales qualified lead to send to Sales for follow-up.

Also, the deals tend to be a lot smaller.  According to authors Aaron Ross and Jason Lemkin in the book *From Impossible to Inevitable*, how hyper-growth companies create predictable revenue, the average sales opportunity of an outbound lead is ten times the size of an inbound lead.

## Outbound lead generation program

To grow and build your business, if you are seeking $5K+ a sale, you won't be able to rely on just inbound to scale.

Outbound lead generation is a more proactive way of generating leads. Depending on the size of your sales team, you may want to split or even outsource your prospecting team and manage in-house your close team.

Prospecting, can be the form of outbound calling, emailing to a cold list (although in Canada and many other countries that is now forbidden without prior consent), events, tradeshows, or by reaching out through social media channels to directly message contacts.  Considered a numbers game, it's important that you effectively manage resources to ensure pipelines are filled and a process can be measured and repeatable.

**Pros**: As you are proactively going after the accounts or prospects, you are deciding who you want to do business with.  As mentioned earlier, deal sizes tend to be a lot larger than those coming from inbound sales.

With accessibility of information on the Internet, in addition to LinkedIn, it's easy to find contact information, changes in personnel, account profiles, news releases, industry trends, etc.

With the explosion of social media more sales opportunities are being cultivated through social selling. A LinkedIn sales navigator platform, you can easily launch a social selling campaign, account information can be gathered and contacts inMailed to start a conversation.

**Cons:** With the pandemic, outbound selling has become more challenging. More people are working remotely and can't be reached through the main phone line, as well as tradeshows and live events are being canceled or becoming virtual.

Harder to close than inbound, your advances are not always well received by prospects and can be damaging to the brand if not done well. It can be very time consuming, determining which accounts to target, identifying decision-makers, gathering contact information, acquiring lists and training a team to proactively and consistently reach out and systematically follow-up with opportunities. Furthermore, with the recent pandemic, contactless selling makes it much more difficult to cultivate relationships.

If you rely on all the salesperson to develop and execute without Marketing support the messaging and marketing material may be off brand, email communication may be spammy and with no and CRM system in place, salespeople can easily walk away with your leads and contacts.

Starting with your sales goals and who your buyers are, will help you decide which lead generation program to launch first. Many businesses focused on high growth, will have a combination of both.

## Use Channels More Likely to Convert into Sales

Not all channels will perform equally in generating quality leads or in attracting website visitors that convert into buyers. There's a lot of data that can help guide you on where best to invest your marketing dollars. And, as mentioned earlier, mapping out your persuasion sequence across multi-touch points, is deemed to be more effective at building your brand and driving conversions than focusing on one channel.

Below is a chart Marketo[xi], a leading marketing automation service provider compiled from their users. The darker shade indicates where leads converted at a higher rate. The first column is the acquisition channel where leads were sourced. The second column shows the average conversion rate percentage of each channel. The third column shows normalized conversion rate so you can do a fair comparison of the data across channels (for example Paid Marketing converts 2x more than Events).

| Acquisition Channel | Conversion Rate - Lead to Opp | Conversion Rate (normalized) |
| --- | --- | --- |
| Sales Prospecting | 0.90% | 0.31 |
| Email | 0.55% | 0.19 |
| Inbound | 3.82% | 1.30 |
| Event | 1.48% | 0.50 |
| Paid Marketing | 2.98% | 1.01 |
| Webinar | 1.61% | 0.55 |
| Nurture | 0.58% | 0.20 |
| Referral | 10.99% | 3.74 |
| Partner | 4.54% | 1.54 |
| Social Media | 1.95% | 0.66 |

It demonstrates what many already know, referrals are your best source of leads, and customers that come to you (inbound by calling or filling out a form) are more likely to close. How to fill your sales funnel with inbound leads, is covered under Harness the Expertise in Creating Great Content and The Power of SEO.

Also, the chart above shows email doesn't convert as well and lead nurture even less.  But one thing to consider is the cost to acquire. If you have built up an opt-in email list, sending 1 or 100 emails the cost doesn't change, whereas a webinar requires a lot more resources to create, market to and follow-up. Keep in mind, the cost to acquire the sale needs to be added to the equation when building and optimizing your sales funnel.

## Increase Lead Conversion with Data Capture

The more you know about your prospects and buyers the greater chance you are at making them sales ready. Here are six ways data capture can help you fill your sales funnel and drive lead conversion.

First you need to decide what's important to them. Knowing their name is important, what about their hobbies, interests and aspirations or their business challenges and pain points?

Potential buyer information can come from your CRM system, billing, sales reps, and sales channels. You can also get information through surveys, contests, form submissions and social media profiles.

In addition to explicit information, online behaviour can be gathered through marketing tools – how and what do they search for online, what channels do they respond to, what pages and sites do they visit and what social media sites do they engage in?  This can allow you to respond with real-time marketing messages that are personalized to their needs.

**Being relevant** is key – the content, offer, product or service must be meaningful to the individual you are trying to connect with or don't start the conversation.

**Personalization** becomes easier with marketing automation tools. With progressive profiling – you never need to ask the customer or prospect for the same information twice but rather continue to ask additional information from online properties to build your contact's profile.

**Capture qualifying information**. Depending on what your ideal client looks like and the triggers that will drive them to buy will help guide you to identifying what information you need to capture for sales-ready opportunities. Consider the importance of their job title in relation to their ability and authority to make decisions, the industry challenges and the lingo or language they may use.

**Be transparent.** The intent of why you are gathering the information needs to be clear and never abused. Having a clear, accessible online privacy policy becomes an important part of your communication to build trust. And if you're not using the information don't ask for it nor collect it.

Finally, deciding to personalize should be based on a decision of security and confidence. The data needs to be accurate as well as meet all legal, regulatory, and risk-averse guidelines otherwise it can impact your reputation and your ability to market.

Even though confidence is slipping, people are still willing to give personal information. The better the incentive the more willing they are. According to a Canada Post survey, 57% of consumers will give their personal info for cash, 33% for relevant offers, 28% for an iPad and 15% when no incentive was offered.

# Design Landing Pages and Websites that Convert Visitors into Buyers

Having a website is an essential marketing asset. However, driving all your visitors to the home page may not get the results you are looking for. Here we outline the importance of having a landing page, tips for converting visitors into sales opportunities and a follow-up persuasion sequence you can implement after they leave your site.

## Landing and Squeeze Pages

Crafting an offer to capture the visitor and convert them into a sales-ready lead or buyer is an art and science. Although a website is important in establishing you as a business and building your reputation, more is needed to control the conversation and direct them to the next desired action.

Remember every communication is an opportunity to lead them to the next step down the sales funnel. This is where landing pages and sometimes referred as squeeze pages are the central point and key element when mapping out the digital sales journey.

A landing page directs the visitor through a series of steps to convince them to buy your product or to convince them to exchange contact information for content.  The squeeze page is different than a landing page, whereas the visitor has nowhere to jump off or link to that carry them off the page. Also, there's no navigation bar on the top or bottom footer.


## Tips to Convert Visitors on Your Page

In working to having a captive audience and to convert them on your landing page, here are some tips:

**Track the source of your traffic** – know where the visitor is coming from (google ad, Facebook post, etc.) and align their expectation on what they find on the page. With all the effort to get them there, you don't want them to bounce off without converting.

**Communicate your value proposition** – above the fold (what they see when they land before they scroll), clearly communicate your value proposition, the compelling reason why you are unique and why they should care.

**Provide proof points and benefits to support your claim** – you can refer to the section on *Website Content List* for helping create the content on your page.

**Have a strong call to action** – whether it's an eCommerce or a lead generation page, you need a strong call to action to convert them. Below are some guidelines for each.

**eCommerce pages** – every panel or scrolling section, have a call to action. If you want them to buy a product, give options or suggestions, discounts, time limited promotions, similar products of interest, past products they viewed, online chat, phone number to call or a go to cart button to click. Never lose the opportunity to offer them a call out - an action to keep them engaged and motivated to buy.

**Lead Generation pages** – the same rule applies. Have a call to action as the visitor scrolls down. Make it clear what they will be receiving, use each panel to tell the story of what you're offering. Keep in mind as the reader scrolls down and spends more time on the page, it increases their likelihood they will exchange their information to sign-up for packaged content. Each panel needs to build on the narrative of why they should act. It can be in the form of benefits, reviews, testimonials, bonuses, time-limited content. Hyperlinks can lead to more content down the page, but don't lead them off the page. Have the online chat or forms as pop-ups or within the panels.

**Online chat** – according to Finances Online a Software Discovery and Research Platform, online chat is used more often for sales than customer support especially for B2B, 85% of the time it's used to manage sales enquires and 74% for B2C. It's also popular for eCommerce sites. If you don't have the resources, third parties are willing to manage your online chat 24/7 at very affordable rates. A great option for small businesses.

## Elements to Test on Your Landing Page:

No persuasion sequence can be optimized without doing an a/b test. A/B testing is when you test different elements on a page, splitting the website traffic to go to different pages and monitor how the pages perform. Based on where you get the conversions, you refine and continue to test new elements against the best performing page. Remember when you create the test, only test one element at a time so you can narrow in on what is causing the change in behaviour.

Here are a few things to test:

- Unique value proposition – what messaging best pulls in getting your potential buyer to act
- Call to action – how you ask, where you position the button and even the colour of the call-to-action button can have enough impact on the quality and volume of sales as well as the cost to acquire a new lead.

- Imagery – it can be powerful in pulling in and driving engagement, don't overlook its impact and ability to entice
- User experience – if your buyer struggles in navigating through your site, he will abandon it quickly and move on
- Offer – ensure you have a compelling offer. Check your competition and what their offering

## Fill Your Website with Content that Achieves Your Business Goals

There are many types of content you need to include if you want to build an impactful website that accurately represents your brand and achieves your business goals. Whether you realize your website desperately needs a facelift or perhaps you launched a new business or product, this is a good time to review your website content. We have compiled a checklist of the types of content you'll need to start telling a compelling and engaging story that drives engagement. The important first steps are to determine the business and communication goals before jumping into wireframes or website designs.

Once you have defined your goals and target audience then it's time to gather your content.



## Branding

- Guidelines
- Logo, brand colours and fonts
- Tagline, unique value proposition

## Product information

- Product categories
- Product descriptions
- Demonstrations
- Pricing models
- Catalogues
- Spec sheets
- Cheat sheets

## Credentials

- Awards
- Certifications
- Testimonials (written, videos)
- Top clients
- Portfolio of work
- Partners/affiliates

- Site/ projects
- Team and their bios

## Social media platforms

- LinkedIn, Google+, Facebook, Twitter, Instagram

## Lead generation

- Contact Us information
- Subscription centre
- Newsletter sign-ups
- Pop-ups
- Webinars
- E-books

## Other available content

- Blogs
- Press releases
- Newsletters
- Videos
- SlideShare
- Calculators
- Whitepapers
- Infographics

**When gathering your content, keep in mind the following**

- Know your competition
- Profile and personas of your audience and how they consume information
- Ranked keywords (how people search for your services)
- Languages (is it a multi-lingual and or multi-regional site?)

Before designing or refreshing your site, make sure you have a marketing strategy and plan in place to ensure your website contributes to the over-arching business strategy.

**Avoid Costly Mistakes in Designing Your Website**

Your website is the face of the company to your audience. It's intended to build the reputation of your business as well as capture and influence your buyers. It's a lost opportunity for your business to use it like a business card or brochureware and to not spend the time, effort, and resources to make it a professional marketing tool.

A website is an important investment in your business. In the chart below, research shows a company's website is the first-place buyers go to seek professional services. We review six costly mistakes to avoid when designing your website:

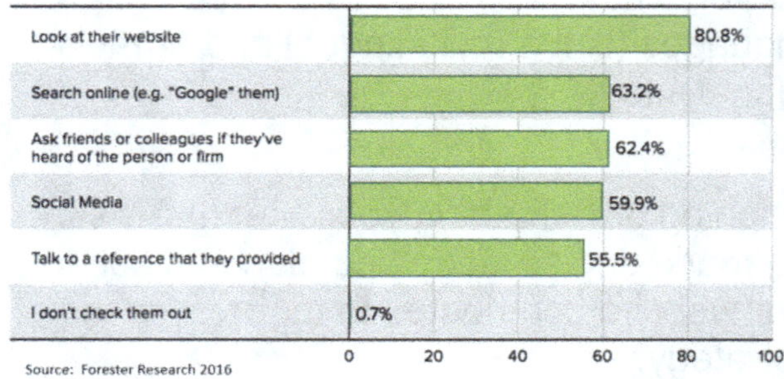


## Poor Quality Images

It's great to have images of your products, but if the lighting is poor, a bad angle or the resolutions isn't right, it's time to invest in a professional photographer. Purchasing quality images may be a better option, although less original and you'll need to make sure you have the usage rights. Also popular is having animated images created to tell your story.

## Long Loading Times

If it takes more than 5 seconds to load your website when someone clicks on it or enters it into Google, you not only lose the interest of the person searching for your type of business but also Google will penalize you. Long loading times is because your images take up too much memory.  Reducing their memory size will increase your loading time. Ask your web designer or developer to check the size of your images.

## Typos

Nothing looks unprofessional like typos. We all have encountered typos when we're sure we've proofread the content a thousand times. Having an editor review your content is priceless.

## Too Much or Too Little Copy

Yes, your site can suffer from both. Too little copy and you lose out on grabbing the interest of your buyer, too much and you can overwhelm them.  A general rule is to figure out the information needs of your customer. Generally, business websites use copy, illustrations, and icons to help the visitor skim through the pages. Read more buttons offer visitors more in-depth information than what is provided on the page. Also using larger font size and colours will make key points stand out.

## Poor Design

The topic of website design can take-up a whole library of books. Design is critical to the whole user experience.  At 360 Integral Marketing, we commonly see small businesses choosing platforms like WIX website builder. It may be easier in the beginning, but we find businesses grow out of these sites as their reputation and brand become more important and businesses more complex. They seek more customization and quality design, that are better suited to a professional business. Furthermore, they grow to learn the importance of attracting traffic through search engine optimization and social media marketing which can be restrictive when using these website builders.

## Making it Hard to Do Business with You

When buyers visit a website and can't figure out what the business is or how to get in touch with someone, you are telling the buyers their business isn't wanted. Making it easy for them to get to know you, what you offer and how to contact you, signals to buyers that you understand them and care to provide the right solutions to meet their needs. Don't forget to take the opportunity to tell them why your business is different right up front. Avoid having the customer search for the answer, have the information available right when they land on your home page. This will make for a happy customer experience and ultimately, lead to more sales.

When customers want to do business with you and share their confidential information, it's important that you have a secure site. SSL certification (Secure Sockets Layer) has become the new norm. It's a bit of code on your web server that provides security for online communications. How you can tell if a website is SSL certified is by looking at the URL in the browser. All websites with an SSL certification start with httsp:// versus http://. Some visitors may be blocked with an error message when they try to log onto the site, leaving a bad first impression.

## Not Mobile Responsive

Today more online browsing starts with a mobile device. If your website is not mobile responsive, the content is distorted, too hard to read or the site won't load at all, you are quickly falling behind your competitors with an unprofessional online presence.

# Use Demand and Lead Generation to Fill Your Sales Funnel

## Lead Generation Versus Demand Generation

If you are looking to fill your sales funnel it's important to know the difference between demand generation versus lead generation. Here, we'll look at the goal of lead generation and demand generation, how they differ, ways to measure success and why they should both be a critical part of your plans in filling your sales funnel.

**Lead Generation:** The goal is to create sales-ready opportunities by collecting information on prospects for sales follow-up; a marketing database can help gather lead information and pass warm leads over to Sales to close. KPIs can include, appointment setting, requests for quotes, proposals, or referrals.

**Demand Generation:** Its goal is to create awareness and demand for an organization's products or services aligned with the mindset of the buyer. The content provided is within the context of who you are targeting and their buying journey. It's not about rushing to close a sale or having them commit to providing their contact information in exchange for content. Demand generation is about disseminating free content across channels to attract new prospects, build brand ambassadors, generate referrals, and reinvigorate interest among potential buyers that may have lost interest. If orchestrated right, it will eventually lead to a sale and more loyal customers.

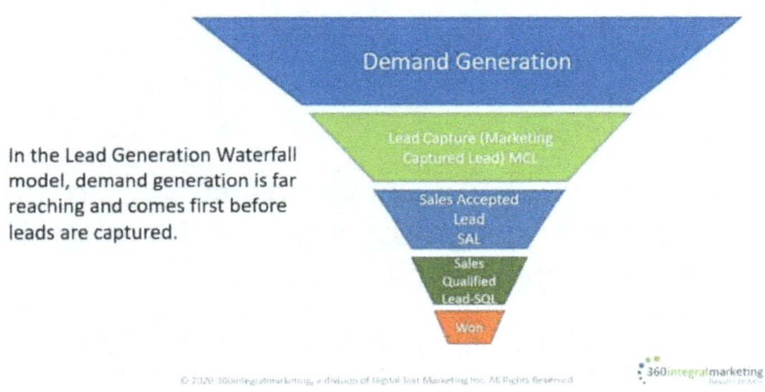



## When to Choose Demand Generation Over Lead Generation?

Demand generation can be used at the top of the funnel when there's little knowledge of your brand or services. This is when you need to invest in inbound marketing and great content marketing to attract, engage and delight. But demand generation is not limited to pulling in opportunities at the top of the funnel. It can also be used to reinvigorate stale leads, lost sales opportunities and leads that were passed to Sales but not yet qualified or sales ready. This is where a demand strategy takes on lead nurturing. Lead nurturing makes a big difference in requalifying and taking a "maybe" or "no" to a "yes".

There are several elements that go into building a well-oiled demand generation machine. If you narrow it down, there's three things to consider:

- **Data insights** on your buyers, what content they would be engaged in
- **Sales-ready website** to point your potential buyers to
- **Marketing automation platform** to run your campaigns and evaluate its progress

## Get More Sales by Nurturing Your Leads

Lead nurturing is when you develop a process to build your relationship with buyers at every stage of the sales funnel.

To start lead nurturing you need a database of potential buyers. If you are starting out it's best to spend your marketing dollars on filling your sales funnel from the top to create a stream of leads for

Sales to follow-up. A more established or mature business would be able to mine their database that may consist of prospects, past and current customers, and stale leads.

How much you invest in lead nurturing also depends on the type of industry. The longer the sales cycle, the higher the revenue opportunity and greater number of stakeholders in the decision-making process, the more important lead nurturing becomes, especially with account-based marketing.

### Building a Prospect Database for Lead Nurturing

In building a prospect database for lead nurturing you will need a marketing automation platform that integrates with your CRM platform. This enables lead information to be passed from Marketing to Sales.

In building a prospect database, the buyers' journey of content can be sent by email based on a set of criteria:

- Source of lead
- Page visits (interests)
- Firmographics (i.e., geography, vertical and/or title)
- Prospect or customer
- Behaviour (opening emails, CTR, etc.)

## Compelling Content that Captivates and Converts Buyers

Content Marketing Starts the Sales Cycle

We talked earlier about identifying the pain points of your buyer and creating solutions that will help solve their problems. Solutions are what people buy and knowing how to position the product to address those pains are important. No longer can businesses focus on pushing products rather it's about providing solutions.

Think about content marketing as an integral part of your demand, lead generation and thought leadership go-to-market plan. It's the best way to help you overcome the challenges of selling your products and services. Content marketing is designed to inform, engage, and entertain and most of all, tell a compelling story on how your products and services can solve business challenges.



**Audience Engagement & Retention** – engaging content has a way of bringing people together and keep them coming back. It's an opportunity to capture their attention and leave a lasting impression.

**Builds Trust** – establishing trust with your target audience takes time and care. When you remain active with your audience and provide relevant content to educate and solve problems, trust is gradually built.

**Shifts Buying Behaviour** – content is a great way to nurture your client along the sales funnel and provide answers to questions, and solutions to problems at every point from the awareness stage right through to purchase,

**Improves Online Ranking & Authority** – the more high-quality content you produce, with a focus on search engine optimization and keyword inclusion, the higher you will be ranked by Google algorithms and your content will be served up more often when your business topics are searched. And, if your business is established as a credible source for information, this will also help you build trust and position yourself as a leader within your industry.

**Pulls in Your Social Media Audience** – there's no better place than social media to share your story. This is where you can promote your brand and share information that is meaningful to your audience. Quality content will help you build trust, a loyal following and potentially a future customer.

## Content to Fill Your Sales Funnel

Depending on how innovative the product is will determine the type of content needed to persuade the audience to move across the sales funnel. A new concept may take longer to sell than a product in an established market. The content they seek and consume will indicate the stage of the buying journey they are at.

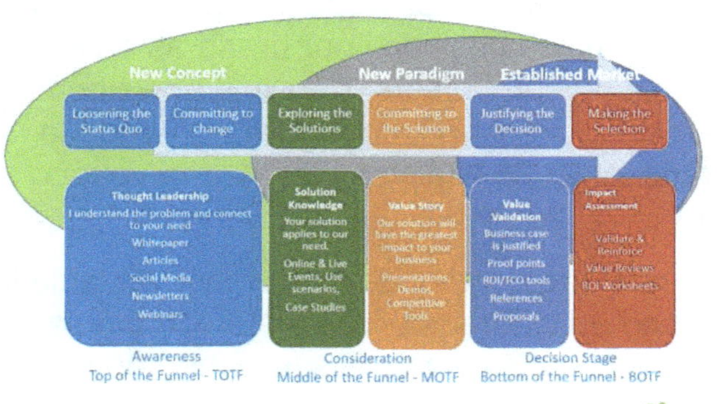

# Empower Your Buyer

Great content is about empowering your buyer to solve their problems by providing advice and solutions, handling objections, making it engaging, entertaining and shareable. Here we provide tips on how to write great content so you can become a marketing genius.

## Know Your Audience

Before you begin to write great content, you'll need to know your target audience. for your digital sales funnel. Writing credible, unique, and thought-provoking content is essential in persuading buyers to buy. Releasing industry-specific and enriching information helps position your brand as an industry leader among competitors. Knowing how your buyers and industry influencers search and the keywords they use is also a vital part of your content strategy.

Determining the content deemed most valuable is also based on where your buyers are in the sales funnel, the complexity of the sale, whether it's at the top of the sales funnel (TOTF), middle of the funnel (MOTF) or the bottom of the funnel (BOTF) where they are when they're ready to purchase.

## Create Content Gets Read

Buyers value their time and guard their personal information. Although many tools can be used to gauge who, where and when they read your content, the critical step in filling your sales funnel is your potential buyers' willingness to exchange their contact information for your content.

People can instinctively tell the difference between good and bad content. You don't want to lose leads by being caught with irrelevant, poorly written, or inaccurate content. Therefore, you must continually work on it and know the secrets behind what makes great content. This is important no matter the size of your audience or your chosen niche.

## Find Your Style

As part of your brand, your style is one of your most important assets to engage your buyers. Your content should be written in a style that is unique to your brand or personality. It's your brand's voice, and you cannot afford to copy someone else's. If you keep on sounding like everyone else, you will find it difficult to add to the ideas of others and contribute to conversations.

While it may be helpful to try other brands' writing techniques as a learner, one of the hallmarks of generating content is establishing your unique style. Once you have found a unique style, you should stick to it and let it evolve.

### Learn to Match Content-Length and Depth

*"Content is anything that adds value to the reader's life" ... Avinash Kaushik*

Experts in generating content have mastered the art of matching the length of their content to the depth of what they want to discuss. Your writing will be all over the place if you try to cover more details than space allows. Similarly, not giving out enough detail despite having space means your content will be watery and boring. The optimal length and depth vary based on the type of content you choose to write and your digital sales funnel objectives. The big idea is to find out what types of content your target audience reads and write the length and depth that's sufficient to engage them.

## Be Good with Research

Great writers are great researchers. While you are always encouraged to be original, you cannot produce top quality content without checking out information from other sources. So being good with research is most essential. Integrating a variety of research will make your content more informative and convenient, eliminating the need for buyers to keep browsing the web for knowledge on a topic. You must know how to research the web to gather reference materials and not just browse the internet. That's what sets your content apart from everyone else and provides the value your buyers are seeking.

## Find a Unique Angle to Every Topic

Great content doesn't follow the crowd. This is not to say that every single topic you write about must be unique. This is impossible since almost every subject of discussion has likely been covered in one form or the other by someone in the past.

The goal is to always find your specific point of view and write from that viewpoint. This is known as the slant of your content. Even when you are covering a trending topic that many content writers have written about, if you'll add to the conversation, then you must find your unique angle. This gives your readers an innovative point of view on a topic, which sets you apart from competitors and makes buyers intrigued in gaining access to your content. If you can't find a unique slant for your content, then it's best you talk about something else entirely.

### Craft a Stunning Introduction

One of the unspoken rules of content writing is to make the first sentence of your write-up your best. This is especially important if you choose to give buyers a short preview of your content. Typically, you only get about three seconds to hook your readers and get them interested enough to want the full content and read on. You must make those precious seconds count and the only way to do that is to hook your readers with a stunning introduction or lead.

For a short article, craft the first paragraph or two in a way that captures the reader's attention. For an e-book, the quality of your first section will determine if the reader reads on or not. You can start with an intriguing question, a little-known fact, the promise of new information or a contrary point of view. Make your lead as compelling as possible and make sure it's appropriate for the type of content you chose to write. It should tease the content of your article without giving away too much about it.

## Be Original – Never Copy

A good content writer never copies. Plagiarism is one of the most grievous offences any writer can commit. It can even impact your sales funnel by making buyers lose trust in you and become hesitant to share their contact information and associate with you. One of the ways to avoid plagiarism is to use an online plagiarism checker. You should aim for a one hundred percent uniqueness score, or close to it.

## Your Content Must Have Value

*"These days, people want to learn before they buy, be educated instead of pitched" … Brian Clark*

The value of your content determines the quality of the writer's skills. No matter the topic or subject of discussion, your readers want to read relevant, accurate and reliable information. Don't over-flog a subject matter or hype information.

Good content always presents accurate information. You shouldn't bend or stretch the truth. People will only see you as an authority in your field when your content has consistently proven to be accurate. For a digital sales funnel, it's important to focus on the information your target audience wants. Don't fill your write-up with irrelevant information. If you are aligned with your audiences' needs and wants, then they will be more interested in your content and your products. You should also provide references to surprising facts and figures quoted in your article. This will make it easy for people to believe what you have to say.

## 7 Best Types of Content to Persuade Buyers

In preparation for creating content, ensure priorities, and timelines, are understood and necessary resources are on hand. When selecting the content to create, consider the following types.

### 1. Blogs

A blog is typically shorter (500-700 words) and provides a quick reference for information. It may not require as much depth, but it's important to keep in mind your business goals when making them. For example, to improve your SEO, blogs are best when keyword rich.

## 2.  Whitepapers

A whitepaper is longer with more detailed information on a particular subject. It's best for sharing innovative, unique viewpoints on a topic that sets you apart from competitors. Since whitepapers have more in-depth information, they can be used to acquire new leads in your digital sales funnel.

## 3.  e-Books

Typically, e-Books vary in length depending on how much detail is needed to cover a topic. It's like a whitepaper but with less data. e-Books are great content to exchange for contact information.

## 4.  Case Studies

This content is best for B2B situations. They are usually shorter forms of content that detail how you solved your client's problem.

## 5.  Infographics

Since these are more visual, it's important to keep the writing brief, with less depth and let the images speak for themselves.

## 6.  Templates & Checklists

This content has proven to be a strong lead generation magnet. They are great resources users will utilize repeatedly and aren't costly to create.

## 7.  Videos

Videos are not always considered written content, but with the growth in popularity and many videos viewed on mute (on Facebook alone, 85% of videos are watched without sound), having a script that follows what is being said increases the likelihood that content will be consumed either through watching, listening, or reading.

One of the most rewarding aspects of developing a successful digital sales funnel is in writing great content. However, creating valued content that is read and shared is an ongoing process. As the market changes so do preferences, how, where and who buys all impact what content is relevant and meaningful. No matter the type of content, knowing the secrets of writing great content will ensure greater success across all stages of your digital sales funnel.

## How Content Can be Optimized to Attract More Buyers

When you know your customer, SEO becomes the driver for earned media and content on your web pages, blogs, and social media platforms. After all Google isn't the only search engine available, YouTube and Twitter are also considered powerful search engines.

The key to unlocking your keyword potential is gaining a full view of how your content is performing across all your web pages and social media platforms and how it attributes to your sales' revenue.

The content you produce must be optimized with the right SEO keywords to be found. Do you have a content strategy that educates, informs, persuades, and solves the problems your potential buyers are seeking? Using the same keywords your target audience is searching for will increase the likelihood of them finding your content.

All communications need to be integrated so the search engines, your website, social media links and content are all working to engage with the buyer and to drive revenue for your business.

Your marketing team or digital experts can help you select the best keywords for SEO, develop great content, and build a dashboard to track your success.

**What you need to monitor to know if your SEO content strategy is working:**

- Traffic and conversions
- Ranking position for keywords and which page or pages are ranking
- Search volumes for keywords (both broad match and exact match)
- Opportunities to further optimize keywords
- Changes implemented and how they impact position, traffic from organic search, and most importantly conversions. (If there are positive changes, look to create some additional content that includes the keywords and continue to watch for changes)
- Links to social media and to your site with optimized keywords
- As frequently as possible, look for other non-branded keywords that can drive organic search traffic and conversions

Remember don't over-optimize or limit your success with only a few keywords. Keep building your business with relevant content that transforms your clicks into sales!

# Challenges Content Marketing Overcomes Down the Sales Funnel

## Competing Solely on Price

If your products or services are considered a commodity, your buyers' decision is all based on price. To reduce price sensitivity, your buyers need to perceive you as having superior services with an investment to help address their challenges. To keep your business top of mind, and build trust with your buyers, the content should be written with the following in mind:

- Position the business as a thought leader in the industry
- Create relevant and timely content across the right audiences to address their potential pain points
- Deliver ongoing communication programs to keep you top of mind among key stakeholders in the buying process
- Provide your sales channel with tips, comparative analysis, testimonials, and case studies to sell more effectively

Buyers are not waiting for your call to solve their problems. More than 70% of buyers will research and decide what companies they want to do business with before they ever talk to a sales representative. Content easily found and well-distributed helps the buyer make the decision during the early stages of the buying cycle. Here are a few ways to expand buyer reach:

- Build-up prospect and client databases with opt-in email addresses to send timely content
- Expand social media (Twitter, Facebook, and LinkedIn etc.) campaigns to reach out to engage followers and encourage social share
- SEO optimize your web site to capture organic searches
- Use Google and Facebook Remarketing campaigns – to reinforce the brand and drive action

Example of a content strategy for a manufacturer of digital equipment:

**Digital Media to Fill Your Sales Funnel**

Digital media continues to play an ever-increasing role in how we entertain ourselves, keep informed, and select the products and services we want to buy. When filling your sales funnel, it's important to be aware of three types of Digital Media and how they are used to drive brand awareness, engagement, and sales conversion.

We will first look at the media types, then dive deeper into the critical role they play at each stage of the buying journey.

## Owned Media

Owned media is what you have more ownership and control over. These are channels and marketing assets you invested in to push out your content and build your narrative around your brand, products, and services. Owned media can include your company's website, your social media company pages, and YouTube channel.

## Paid Media

Paid media is when you pay a third party to push out and spread the word about your brand, products, and services. The impact it has on your sales funnel is more direct, immediate, and measurable. Examples of paid media are PPC Campaigns, Display Ads and Programmatic Advertising.

**Earned Media**

Earned media is powerful and considered more credible as it isn't seen as paid or a controlled media narrative by your company. Because it's considered more organic, it can take time before you realize its rewards. Furthermore, you may not always be able to track back the investment or the impact it has on acquiring new business. Examples of earned media include search engine optimization, influencers or industry leader, endorsements, testimonials and reviews about your brand products or service.

# PPC Campaigns

### What are PPC Campaigns?

Are you wondering about the different types of PPC Campaigns out there to fill your sales funnel? Or perhaps you're wondering what is PPC? We cover the basics to help you get started.

### What Is PPC?

PPC stands for Pay per Click. PPC marketing campaigns build your online presence and fill your digital sales funnels. It's an important part of your digital marketing strategy and a quick way to generate traffic to your website. Done right it successfully fends off your competition while driving demand for your company, products, services, events, contests, content and more.

## How Does it Work?

When a visitor clicks on your advertisement to go to your landing page or website, you pay the advertiser for each time the ad is clicked. The amount may vary based on how your competitors bid for the same ad placement. This auction happens in real-time.

## How Much Does It Cost?

The cost to manage a campaign can vary. Expect to pay for the following:

**Campaign creative** – creative development, ad copy, landing page design and copy

**Campaign set-up** – daily/monthly maximum budget, maximum cost per bid, keywords, audience segments, search engines, social media platforms, campaign reporting

**Ongoing management and optimization** – online marketing at its best requires continuous testing and improving. Nothing stands still.

For Google AdWords, the media buy usually starts at $2,000 a month to get any type of return. How competitive the keywords you're bidding on will drive up or down the costs. It can take up to two-months to optimize results, knowing the right copy, keywords (positive and negative) to fine tune your results. Set-up and management can be a fixed fee or a % of your media buy or a combination of the two. Social media buys are typically less expensive but also less effective if you are trying to capture buyers when they are sales ready. For building demand and awareness Social Media, Google Display and Remarketing are recommended. Check out *Display and Programmatic Advertising* to learn how Display can effectively drive demand.

## Calculating Your Conversions

There are many variables that will determine how well you are able to get your target audience to click on your ads and from there turn them into a buyer. We recommend before you embark on running a PPC campaign to put together a business case, deciding what would be a reasonable volume of traffic and on-page conversion you can generate from your PPC campaign.

Below gives you a guideline of how the different types of PPC campaigns can perform across platforms in driving traffic to your site. Keep in mind these are just averages, and the KPIs can change based on the competitive landscape. When you know your marketing costs and gross margins, you'll also be able to calculate your MROI (marketing return on investment). Once a person lands on your page, the conversion from them becoming a visitor to a lead can vary greatly from 2 -10%.  How well you design the page, and the source of traffic will impact those numbers. For eCommerce on page conversion, it averages about 1-3%.

## PPC CAMPAIGN KPIs

| CAMPAIGN TYPES | Average KPIs* |
|---|---|
| Google AdWords | CPC = $1.00 -$2.00<br>CTR = 2- 3%<br>CPM = $35 |
| Google Display Ad Campaigns | CPC = $.25<br>CTR = .5%<br>CPM = $2.80 |
| Facebook/Instagram Campaign | CPC = $.64<br>CTR = 1.20%<br>CPM = $7.77 |

*Averages may vary based on industry, geography, seasonality and products.

PPC Campaign KPIs

**CPC:** Cost-Per-Click is the cost you pay the platform every time a potential buyer clicks on your ad.

**CTR**: Click-Thru-Rate is the percentage of times someone clicks on your ad when it's displayed. The higher the CTR, the more effective your ad is generating traffic to your site.

**CPM:** Cost-Per-Thousand, is the cost you pay per thousand views. If the CPM is $7.00, you are paying $7.00 for 1000 people to view your ad. This KPI becomes more important when purchasing display or programmatic advertising and you are seeking to generate brand awareness.

**Google PPC Campaigns**

Google Ads for PPC

This type of PPC Campaign is one of the most popular whether you're a small business or a big brand. With the volume of searches on Google, that's where you'll find most of your buyers.

How to Set it Up

To set-up a Google Ads campaign [xii], you need to gather the following:

- Keywords your potential buyers will use to search for your type of products or services
- Where your buyers are located

- Who are your competitors?
- Ad copy
- A landing page to send them to
- A phone number if you want them to call from a mobile ad
- Your budget – how much are you willing to spend?
- A follow-up process – how will the leads or sales be managed internally?

Google Ads appear either at the top of your screen or the side or bottom of the page of SERP (Search Engine Results Page). With Google, they will have an AD icon so those searching will know that a business had purchased the spot to display the ad. If a business is displayed on a page and it's not an ad, then that is referred to as an organic placement versus a paid search placement. Research has shown that, although the organic search is more likely to be clicked on, when someone does click on an ad, they are more intent on buying.

You can set target locations, allocate a maximum bid and a maximum monthly budget when setting up your ads.

How much to bid will be based on how much your competitors are also willing to pay for the same ad placement. The number of estimated clicks or your target goal and the bid amount will determine your budget.

When one clicks on your ad it's called a click-through rate (CTR) and it is based on how many times your ad was viewed on the page over how many impressions the ad received. Each industry's average CTR varies but is typically 2%; above 2% is considered above average.

Google Display Network for PPC

Google's online advertising technology allows you to advertise with text and image ads on a variety of news sites, blogs, and other niche sites across the internet. The Google display network reaches 90% of Internet users. It generates higher impressions but lower CTR than Google Ads. So, it's important to know what your goals are; is it primarily awareness, leads or sales?

Like setting up a Google Ads campaign, it can start with the keywords based on your key audience, the products, and solutions you offer and your audience types. With the Google Display Network, you'll need to [xiii] create image ads along with text. Your ads will be displayed on the websites that agreed to be part of the network and have similar content, audience types and keywords to those you have chosen.

## How Google Sets Up Your Target Audiences

Refining your target audience and call to action based on interest, habits, what they're actively researching, or how they have interacted with your business is one great way to build your digital sales funnel.

## Your Different Audience Options

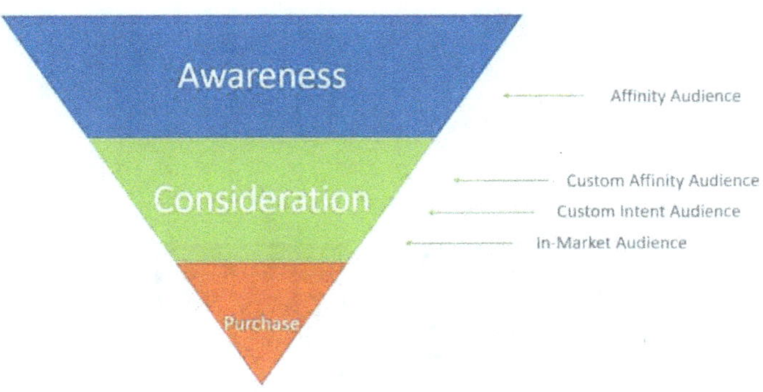


- Affinity audiences
- Custom affinity audiences

- Life events
- In-market audiences
- Custom intent audiences
- Remarketing
- Detailed demographics
- Customer match
- Similar audiences

Like other PPC Campaigns, with Google Ads, you can set-up the campaign based on cost-per-click or cost-per-impression (CPM). The cost is based on every 1,000 impressions.

## Remarketing For PPC

Knowing only 1- 2% of your visitors may purchase or contact you to enquire about your product, investing in a remarketing program is a good option. Remarketing follows your potential buyer after they leave your site or YouTube channel [xiv] and offers them an incentive or reminder to return and purchase your product on your website.

Based on cookie technology, as your potential buyer goes anywhere on the Internet that is part of the ad network, they will be served up an ad that can be targeted to what interests them. Remarketing gets you in front of your buyer giving them a second, third or even a fourth chance to convert. As with other pay-per-click campaigns, it requires bidding in real-time with other businesses for ad placement.

Remarketing is available with Google Ads as well as Facebook. With Apple's IOS upgrades blocking cookies, there will be limited tracking for Facebook to gather learning for serving up such ads.


**Social Media PPC Campaigns**

There are many different social media platforms. Choosing the right platform to generate leads and awareness depends on what channels your target audience engages with and would see the relevance in having your ads displayed there.  Looking at what platforms your competitors have been successful in building a following is a good place to start. Below are the top six social media platforms. For each we will provide some insights into their targeting opportunities.


## Social Media PPC Campaigns


- YouTube
- Facebook
- Instagram
- TikTok
- Twitter
- LinkedIn


### YouTube for PPC

YouTube, also managed under Google, has over two billion monthly visitors – and that's just the people who've signed in.

### Here is How it Works:

Select from two types of audiences, In-market, and Affinity [xv], then select your business categories to build your audience profile. (Below is a list of categories for each of the two audiences.) Your audience type helps determine the stage of the sales funnel they are in.

YouTube video ads are within 30-second lengths, and you are billed when someone clicks on the ad or has viewed the ad for the 30 seconds. Except for charging by cost per view, they are set up like the other types of PPC campaigns, as follows:

- Type of ad
- Your bid
- Bidding selection
- Average CPV (Cost Per View)
- Your budget
- Average CPM (Cost per thousand impressions)

## Match Your YouTube Audience to Business Goals and Ad Formats

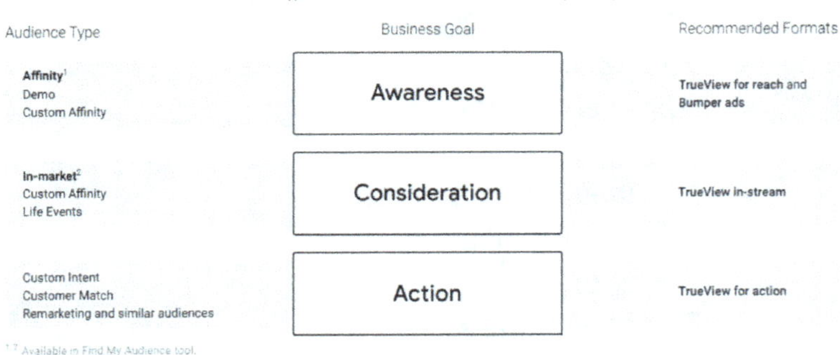


**Source: YouTube**

**Affinity Audience:** this group is more in the awareness stage of your sale funnel, selected based on their interests and habits that relate to your product offer. For more refined targeting you can set-up a custom Affinity audience [xvi].

- Banking & Finance

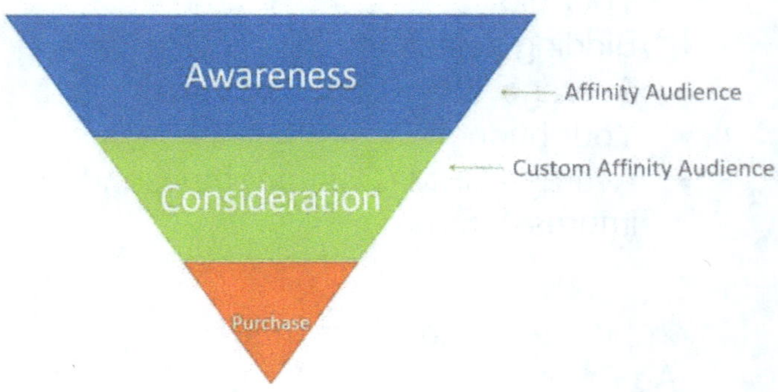


- Beauty & Wellness
- Food & Dining
- Home & Garden
- Lifestyles & Hobbies
- Media & Entertainment
- News & Politics
- Shoppers
- Sports & Fitness
- Travel

**In-Market Audience:** people actively researching or planning to purchase products or services in one of these categories – is in the consideration stage and further down the sales funnel than the Affinity audience.

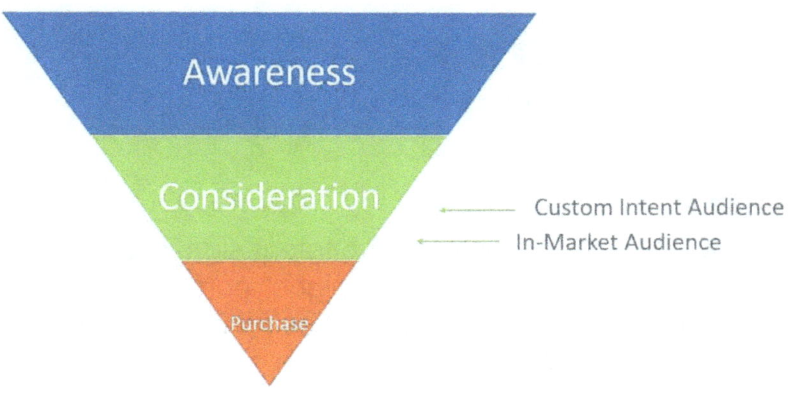


- Apparel & Accessories
- Arts & Crafts Supplies
- Autos & Vehicles
- Baby & Children's Products
- Beauty Products & Services
- Business & Industrial Products
- Business Services
- Computers & Peripherals
- Consumer Electronics
- Education

- Employment
- Event Tickets
- Food
- Gifts & Occasions
- Home & Garden
- Media
- Software
- Sports & Fitness
- Telecom

## Did You Know?

Ads served up with Google Intent signals 30% higher consideration lift and 40% higher purchase intent than when they are serviced using demographic signals alone.

*Google* Brand *Lift*, Global, Smartphone (Analysis Restricted to Smartphone to Isolate the Impact of Targeting), July 2017–June 2018.

Facebook is one of the most powerful among the different types of PPC Campaigns and deemed the largest auction on the Internet. In 2024, the global number of Facebook active users [xvii] is 3.049 billion! Being so data-rich, you can cost-effectively reach your desired audience based on several data elements.

To launch Facebook social media PPC campaigns on Ads Manager, you need to set your maximum daily or lifetime budget and your bid amounts. Facebook, with its rich content, allows you to target based on the following selections:

## Parameters for Selecting Your Target Audience on Facebook:

**Location:** targeted by country, states/regions/provinces, cities (a radius within a city), zip and postal codes

**Demographics**: language, age, and gender

**Interests:** pages they liked and other ad engagement on Facebook

**Behaviours:** based on their digital activities, what devices they use, past or intended purchases, and travel

**Custom Audience**: you can also choose to download a list of customers or choose to retarget potential buyers that visited your site

The next time they go on Facebook, they'll be able to view your ads.

## Facebook Platform Captures Contact Lead Information

Facebook can capture lead information pulling from the user's Facebook profile and sending the lead information for follow-up instead of driving the prospect to a landing page to complete a form. However, the bigger challenge for B2B advertisers on Facebook is generating conversions and high-quality leads. As with many social media platforms, the contact info used is never their business contact information.

## Build your Facebook Campaign Based on Your Objectives

As a powerful social media platform, Facebook offers more than PPC campaigns, with other engagement goals in mind, you can increase brand awareness and popularity. If you want to build your brand for consumer services and products or target small business owners, then this may be worth your investment, but for generating business-to-business leads there may be better alternatives to reach your audience.



Instagram is quickly making headway in the social media market and is useful to businesses. According to Hootsuite, advertisements on Instagram can reach up to 849.3 million people, a worthwhile platform to consider for a PPC Campaign.

Launching a PPC ad campaign on Instagram follows the Facebook process very closely. Using the Facebook Ads Manager, you can select Instagram as an ad [xviii] placement location. This campaign follows the same process as setting up the Facebook PPC Campaign. You can set up your maximum bid, your goals for the advertisement, such as brand awareness, and the target audience. The target audience categories are the same as Facebook's:

- Demographics and location of audience
- Interest and behaviours on and off Instagram
- Custom audiences. A list of people that are already your customers

## TikTok for PPC

TikTok is an emerging social media platform targeting young adults and provides PPC advertising options to businesses. To launch a TikTok PPC ad [xix], you will need to use their Ads Manager. TikTok allows you to target your audience based on:

- Custom audience – like Facebook, this allows you to target customers
- Demographics – age, gender, language
- Consumer interests and behaviours – the content that the users have engaged with previously
- Location – organized by country, province, or city

The cost of using TikTok's PPC campaigning is controllable. Through Ads Manager, you can set a daily or lifetime budget and specify your bidding amount. An interesting feature of TikTok is that it has many affiliated apps, such as Vigo Video, TopBuzz and BuzzVideo, among others. Unlike the other types of PPC Campaigns, you can either specify the app that you would like TikTok to post the ad on or allow TikTok to distribute the advertisement to the most relevant platforms.

## Twitter For PPC

Twitter's PPC Campaigns can be accessed using Twitter Ads. You can choose the goal for your advertisements, such as website clicks or your audience's engagement, among others. If you choose website clicks, then you will be charged based on the CPC method, while the other goals use different costing methods, such as CPM.

Like PPC Campaigns it's an auction model, which means that you're bidding on access to Twitter and your target audience. Twitter has different bidding models that you can choose from and allows you to set budgets for the total amount you're willing to spend during the campaign or the maximum amount you want to spend daily. When setting up the campaign, you can choose the audience you would like to target.

## Your Twitter Target Audience Can be Segmented by the Following:

**Interests**: Twitter has over 350 interest categories to choose from.

**Keywords:** Twitter is a powerful search engine. People use this social media platform to keep updated. Like other campaigns, you can choose specific keywords that they have recently used in their tweets or engaged within tweets.

**Followers**: Reach your audience based on specific interests they have or your followers. Good for targeting niche audiences.

**Television:** Reach people who Tweet about or engage with Tweets about their favourite television shows.

**Demographics:** You can also target by geography, language, gender, and device.

### LinkedIn for PPC

LinkedIn is a social media website for business professionals. Social Media PPC campaigns on LinkedIn offers a choice of ad types on their platform. The precision targeting is as follows:

- Job title and function
- Industry
- Company size
- Specific companies
- Seniority
- Geography

### LinkedIn's Different Ad Types

**Text Ads** have the widest reach but are much less visible on the page. Text ads can be displayed on any page of the platform, on the top, just below the navbar and on the side. The impressions are much higher than a Sponsor Ad but the CTR is much lower.

**Sponsored Ads** are a much larger ad than Text ads. They tend to be more expensive with lower impressions and higher engagement. These ads can also be created by boosting an organic post to a specific audience or created – like Facebook.  Sponsored Content runs on the home page within the newsfeed.

**Sponsored InMail Ads** are ad messages sent to your target audience through the LinkedIn inbox. You bid on what you're willing to pay per send. The message is sent only when the person is logged in and you pay only when the message is sent.



Like Facebook you can choose to capture the contact information from the platform without directing them to a landing page and filling out a form. But the added benefit is you can also pull-in their LinkedIn profile link and load it to your CRM for follow-up.

Like other PPC campaigns, you bid for ad placements. It requires a minimum $10 a day budget and $2.00 per click. It also offers Cost Per Thousand (CPM) views. This platform is especially important for B2B marketing. As of 2021, there are 30 million businesses on LinkedIn and 250 million active users.

Knowing the different types of PPC Campaigns is one step closer to filling your sales funnel.  When you combine them with a test and learn approach you will go far in optimizing your results and getting the best Marketing ROI for your business.

## Jump into the Power of SEO

As we discussed earlier SEO is an important consideration when crafting your content to support demand, lead generation and thought leadership.

Here we'll go deeper into the impact SEO has on generating leads and capturing sales opportunities real-time. SEO can be your gateway to gain access to the customers actively seeking to buy your product or service. It's a way to build organic visitors over time and is considered the most trusted source of traffic. Users trust search engines and achieving a top spot in search engine rankings signals to searchers that your site is a credible source. The higher you rank in results pages, the more clicks and traffic your site will generate. Don't underestimate the power of a search engine and the results it can drive to help fill the sales funnel.

These SEO stats showcase the strength behind using the right words to engage with your audience:

- 68% [xx] of online experiences begin with a search engine
- 3% [xxi] of all website traffic comes from organic search
- 96% [xxii] of global traffic comes from Google search, Google Images, and Google Maps
- SEO drives 1000%+[xxiii] more traffic than organic social media
- 7% [xxiv] of search queries contain four words or more

Finding the right words and phrases consumers are searching for, the type of content they are looking to read and knowing where the conversation is happening is important. And, knowing what content to serve up and to whom at each stage of the sales funnel, will help you narrow down terms, phrases, and keywords consumers are searching.

## What is a SERP and why is it important to SEO?

Search engine result pages also known as SERP [xxv] are web pages served up by search engines like Google when these keywords and terms are searched. SERPs tend to include organic search results, paid Google Ads results, Featured Snippets,

Knowledge Graphs, and Video results. Depending on your digital strategy, or lack of, your business may never appear in the top web pages that are served up. In fact, your business may not appear until two or three web pages into the search.

SEO Best Practices

There are a multitude of things a business can do to integrate SEO into their marketing strategy. But there are a few best practices to elevate the chances of your business being discovered and served up to the top of the web page results. Implement these 7 bests SEO practices to ensure higher website ranking success:

**Word Discovery:** Discover the words, keywords, and phrases your audience is searching for. You can either do this using SEO tools like SEMRush [xxvi], or you can hire an SEO Specialist to help you with this discovery. Don't get caught in the alphabet soup of words without some direction on how to implement it. Although finding keywords is an important first step in your efforts to optimize searches in your favour, it can take several months before a business website moves up in the rankings. A keyword strategy is great for organic growth, but results will amplify more quickly when combined with a paid strategy like social media PPC and Google AdWords campaigns.

**Website Content:** Once you've completed the keyword discovery, it's time to add these words through-out your website. Not only do you want to sprinkle them a few times through-out your site, ensure you mention your keywords at the top of your web pages as Google puts more weight on words at the top of a web page.

**Titles and Descriptions:** Take the time to put titles and descriptions on content placed on your site. This includes image descriptions. Avoiding duplicate content on your site and it will rank higher. This includes not duplicating title tags, meta description tags, eCommerce product pages, landing pages, image alt text and category pages. For eCommerce sites, this is a ton of work, but worth the effort and will prove beneficial with increased traffic and sales.

**Title Tags:** Title tags on-page for SEO is essential. Google has even said it's important to use high-quality titles on your web pages. The best way to do this is to put your keywords right in your title tag as search engines pay close attention to these titles.

**Website Speed:** The site's loading speed plays into the SEO equation. Google puts an emphasis on your ranking based on how quickly the site loads. The quicker the site loads the better it will be ranked. What affects the speed of a site? Images that are not compressed is a big one and can make up the bulk of a page's size and loading speed. WordPress themes can also slow things down if they are not optimized for speed. Use lazy loading images, as this can increase your speed by 50%. Lazy Loading defers the loading of an image that is not needed on the page immediately. An image, not visible to the user when the page loads, is loaded later when the user scrolls and the image becomes visible. If the user never scrolls, an image that is not visible to the user never gets loaded.

**Blog Content:** Newly created content is one of the best ways to raise website rankings organically. The keyword discovery will feed into the blog topics that are most searched. Create new content often. The more you post, the more eyeballs you'll receive, the more you'll want to post. And don't forget to use unique titles and descriptions as pointed out above.

**Google/PPC Campaigns:** It's no surprise when you include paid lead strategies as part of the SEO mix, the faster the leads will flow, and the better your results. Google AdWords, Display, Remarketing and PPC campaigns are most successful when done in tandem. Don't miss the opportunity to do A/B testing, to see what offer or message pulls better and drives more leads. Remember, the keyword discovery at the start will feed into your PPC campaign strategies, providing an added boost to your media spend.

**Mobile Responsive:** For google it's all about providing a relevant and positive online experience. With the growth in mobile users, you're missing out if your website is not mobile responsive. Google will suppress your website from being displayed in mobile searches if it isn't mobile responsive.

There are hundreds of SEO tactics to raise a website ranking on Google and other search engines like Bing to generate more qualified leads for your sales funnel. Both paid and organic strategies are important when driving traffic and brand awareness for your products and services.

## Why SEO is the Best Investment for Generating Targeted Traffic and Increasing Your Profitability

As part of your online business marketing strategy, SEO is critical as it provides the opportunity to capture buyers when they are seeking solutions that your company can provide. With the right search engine marketing experts, they'll enhance your brand by using various digital marketing strategies to generate more leads for your business. Without it, you can hurt your brand if customers are expecting to find you and you're not there.

If you still aren't convinced SEO is worth the time and investment?  Here are 10 more compelling reasons:

1. Organic search had the highest customer conversion rate among all the inbound and outbound marketing channels according to HubSpot reports [xxvii]
2. Internet experiences begin 93% [xxviii] of the time starting with search
3. Search is the number one driver of traffic to content sites [xxix], it generates a lot more volume than social media more than 300% according to Outbrain study
4. SEO leads have a much higher close [xxx] rate than outbound leads (14.6% close rate, while outbound leads (such as direct mail or print advertising) have a 1.7% close rate
5. 70-80% of users never click on paid ads and only focus on the organic results [xxxi]
6. 75% of searchers never scroll past the first page
7. SEO brings in more qualified leads [xxxii] than Pay Per Click or Google AdWords
8. Google controls roughly 70% of the search market and over 90% of mobile searches
9. Yellow Pages are on a rapid decline
10. According to Google, over 50% of consumer searches are to find information about local businesses

SEO pulls in targeted traffic down the sales cycle. Influencing and impacting your buyers' journey requires building your content in partnership with your search terms. The goal is to connect with your buyer at the right time with the right content to acquire more qualified leads and higher sales conversions.

## Jump the Line by Targeting Your Competitors

Becoming a marketing genius can start with working off the competitions coat tails to acquire new customers. With a captive audience and lower cost of acquisition, you can easily jump in and get in front of your competitors' target audience.

The strategy is simple, and quite brilliant. Find your competitor's customers before they get to the purchase stage of their sales funnel.  Imagine that your competitor, let's call them ABC Company, has invested their marketing budget in the early stages of educating the customer about the benefits of their products/services (which happen to be like yours, except for your unique value proposition). If ABC Company has zeroed in on specific keywords, or Google AdWords buys, knowing this information gives you a competitive advantage. And the good news is it won't be as difficult as you may think to sway their intended customer over to you with the right messaging at the right time.

The strategy can be used on a few channels, and it's worth exploring one or more as part of your plan.

**Google AdWords** – there's no better way to get to your competitor's audience than by bidding on their company name. This is a low-cost way to gain high quality AdWords clicks. Brand keywords can prove to be some of the best performing words to target. The best part of this approach is that the buyers who are looking for a particular brand or company are in final stages of their search, which is a perfect time to come in and scoop them up.

**Facebook Ads** – Target your competitor's customers by targeting their interests on Facebook. Facebook offers some of the best customer targeting capabilities around. Do some research on what posts your competitors are using, and serve up something better with your ad. Although Facebook doesn't allow you to specially target fans of competitor pages, they do make it easy to target people with similar interests, all you need to do is enter the competitor's

fan page in the Interests section, and their customers
are now your customers.

**LinkedIn Custom Audience** – Similar to Facebook,
you can create custom audiences who have the
same skills and belong to the same groups as your
competitors. Targeting options include location, job
title, seniority level, gender, and age making it easier
to identify the perfect customer.

**Twitter** – It might go without saying, but whatever
you can do on Facebook and LinkedIn you can do
something similar on Twitter. Follow your
competitor's profile on Twitter and investigate who
their following is. If people are already following the
advice and content of this company, they're primed
to receive a targeted message from your company.

**YouTube Ads** – Imagine your perfect customer is
preparing to watch ABC Company's video on
YouTube and your business's ad pops up right
before theirs plays, how perfect would that be? If
your competitor's video allows monetization, you're
in the best spot to jump in front with your own ad.
Don't want the audience to skip ahead, be sure your
content and creative resonates with them so they
don't even bother watching the competitor's video.

## Display and Programmatic Advertising to Drive Demand

Digital Advertising in the form of display or programmatic advertising is commonly used to generate brand awareness and demand. They can effectively be used at the top of the sales funnel to help engage buyers and make them more sales ready.  According to Forrester Research, interested users are 56% more likely to complete a purchase if they first encounter engaging display advertising before clicking on a search-based ad. The more personal the message, the better your chances. Displaying a compelling ad across platforms with competitive pricing to a potential buyer after viewing your product can be very persuasive in driving opportunities down the sales funnel.

### What Are the Differences?

Both are digital advertisements that use advanced data analytics to place ads real-time.  The key difference is display network advertising takes place on a closed network like the Google Display Network and programmatic advertising involves buying ad space across multiple ad exchanges. With programmatic it's more complex with a much larger inventory, more choices, and players. The benefits of programmatic is the potential reach with access to a massive inventory for placing your ads and is seamlessly displayed on web pages.

## Here are 5 Reasons to use Display and Programmatic Advertising

**Builds Brand Awareness:** Expand your reach and drive a higher volume of traffic. Appear on reputable sites that are popular amongst your intended audience gives you the opportunity to make a great impression.

**Keeps You Top-of-Mind:** If your services and products are not likely to be purchased immediately, your brand can still stay top-of-mind for prospects for when they are considering making a purchase.

**Visually Display Your Products**: They support a lot of ad image sizes and types including video to visually demonstrate your product and brand rather than text-only search ads.

**Adds Coverage**: Expand your reach and get additional keyword and product coverage across websites and platforms.

**Remarkets to Potential Buyers:** After visitors have visited your site or a site with comparable content, you can retarget them to drive them to your site to further engage with your brand and pull them down the sales funnel.

## eCommerce: The Future of Remote Shopping

For many companies' eCommerce has become a critical part of their business growth strategy and this trend will continue. Businesses who once only served customers in person, such as retail outlets, professional services and other service providers are now looking to the eCommerce space to thrive. It's never been a better time to expand your business with a strong eCommerce growth strategy.

### The Social eCommerce Explosion

Online marketplaces are quickly becoming the more popular way to buy products and services. eCommerce trends in 2021 show that for the first time ever, grocery retailers like Target were listed in the top ten according to an eMarketer rating of eCommerce retailers. Traditional retailers are no longer trailing behind in the digital space and are turning to social media and eCommerce to connect with their customers. Brands are growing more accustomed to executing integrated marketing strategies using social media, SEO optimized content and PPC Campaigns as a way to build brands and grow market share.

## Contactless Shopping

Businesses that can turn their process online will do so, and in-person contact will be limited for the foreseeable future. Providing a good/great customer experience will be the main theme along with quality products, and automated, fast free shipping. With social platforms such as Instagram and Facebook already using in-app purchasing tools, brands will benefit from shorter buying cycles and quicker lead conversions.

## Product Selection Skyrockets

eCommerce trends show consumer shopping needs have changed in the past year. eCommerce is providing buyers with almost everything they need without having to leave the comfort of their living room or office. And the list of products is no longer restricted to fashion and gadgets. Product selection has expanded to include groceries, cars, furniture and more.

What was once considered a simple convenience, eCommerce is now essential for any business looking to engage with buyers. Having your products at the top of a buyer's online shopping search will capture 25% of the clicks. However, success is not guaranteed by relying solely on SERPs (Search Engine Ranking Pages). Brands require a 360 integrated marketing approach to build trust, solve the buyer's problems and deliver a positive user experience. For those businesses who are serious about selling online, there is enormous potential if done correctly.

**Omnichannel Experience - the New Norm**

Brands with both a physical and online presence should look to deliver a cohesive omnichannel user experience[xxxiii] at every touchpoint. Understanding the customer's buying journey will help with building effective marketing sales funnels. Having the right platforms and eCommerce infrastructure to promote a great user experience with a well-crafted sales funnel will be the key to success.


# Webinars for Contactless Selling

Wondering how to master the science and art of creating webinars to fill your sales funnel? The popularity of webinars is growing as more businesses rely virtually on filling their pipelines and growing sales. Here's how you make your webinars successful from the top to the bottom of your sales funnel.

*"They take the old teleseminar/speaking model to a whole new level" – Russell Brunson, Dotcom Secrets*

Webinars are one of the most versatile ways of drawing in your audience. They allow you to share engaging content that motivates buyers to purchase your products and services. With many different webinar formats, they never become uninteresting to your buyers. But, like any other content, creating a successful webinar for demand and lead generation must be done carefully and strategically, using the right marketing tactics.

Let's review how to setup webinars and how to promote them to generate demand and leads for your business.

## Why are Webinars Effective at Filling Your Sales Funnel?

Some of the greatest challenges in building your sales funnel is finding high-quality leads and closing deals. With engaging platforms, remote working conditions, and a need to stay informed, webinars' popularity has grown. Webinars have been proven to be an important part of your integrated marketing communications strategy and demand and lead generation. In fact, a 2019 survey revealed that 58% of demand generation [xxxiv] marketers think webinars are "the most successful tactic for top-of-funnel engagement." Also, 48% stated [xxxv] that webinars "move prospects through the rest of the marketing funnel effectively."

## Top of the Funnel

In this stage, the emphasis is on generating awareness and interest. As a sales rep, it's a struggle to get potential buyers to speak with you because they prefer to do their own research before reaching out. However, webinars allow you to combine their research stage with interaction with sales leaders or industry experts. By hosting only one webinar, it has the possibility to generate over 1000 leads [xxxvi] for your company. But what is most interesting is that it doesn't generate just any leads. 73% of B2B marketers [xxxvii] say a webinar is the "best way to generate high-quality leads." Having good quality leads makes you more likely to receive a response from them and close the sale. In such rapidly advancing industries and with highly competitive quotas, webinars can be the key to having a successful sales funnel.

In this stage, the emphasis is on lead nurturing and providing solutions to their problems. It's essential to solidify the trust and relationship that you have already started to form and demonstrate how products like yours can solve their problem. This will help your buyers swiftly move to the bottom of the funnel.

## Goal #1: Sharing Information

When your buyers are trying to gather information about your product, a webinar can give them live Q&A sessions where they can get prompt responses. Also, you can conduct product demonstrations so they can see and hear firsthand how simple and effective your product is.

## Goal #2: Relationship Building

By observing your audience's questions and interactions, you can find out more about them, which helps you personalize your marketing and build better relationships. As you continue lead nurturing, webinars are also useful to generate emotions that influence your buyers. A study revealed[xxxviii] that consumers' subconscious emotions have a large impact on purchasing decisions. So, when you have a webinar that establishes a human connection early on, you will be in a better position to nurture and convert your leads.

## Bottom of the Funnel

In this final stage, buyers are interested in your goods and services, but they need a final nudge to convince them. Using a webinar, can answer your consumers' last questions immediately. Showing live product demonstrations, case studies and discussing your after-purchase support and customer experience are great ways to encourage your buyers to purchase your product. Webinars have been proven to be effective at the bottom of the funnel as well because of their incredible conversion rates. Whereas an email campaign may get a conversion rate of 1-5% [xxxix], a webinar can have a conversion rate of around 20% [xl] – four times as much as the best email campaign.

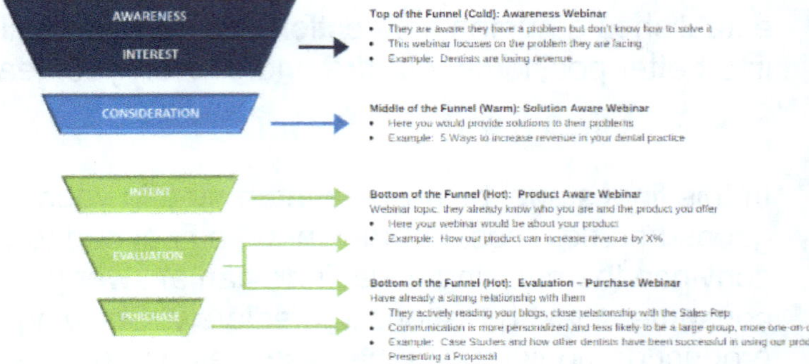


## 7 Key Steps in Creating a Successful Webinar for Demand and Lead Generation

It's evident that webinars play an essential role in all stages of the digital sales funnel for demand/lead generation and conversion. However, if they're not done properly, they can have a negative impact on your business. For example, if you provide untailored or uninteresting content, then you can lose your leads. To avoid these blunders and get the most from your content, here are seven steps for creating a successful webinar:[xli]

### 1. Clearly Define Your Goals

Start by identifying the challenges or opportunities where you're struggling to convert prospects into buyers. Your goals may vary—whether it's generating demand, attracting interest in your product, converting leads into loyal customers, or increasing overall market demand. Defining your goals is crucial because it guides your decisions on target audience, content, and the format of your webinar. With clear objectives, you can align your entire webinar plan to achieve the desired outcomes. This also allows you to effectively measure the webinar's success and make adjustments as needed.

## 2. Understand your target audience

Once you have chosen your goals, it's time to determine your target audience. Consider the industry, specific companies, and who in the organization you are looking to reach. Then, based on this information, you can understand what issues they're facing and what you need to do to solve them. Understanding your target audience will allow you to create relevant and personalized content, product offerings, qualifying questions, and more effective campaigns to promote your webinar.

## 3. Develop content based on your target audience, funnel stage and goals

When creating content, consider your target audience, the stage of the sales funnel they are in, and your specific goals. You might share various types of content, such as information about your products or services, insights into industry challenges, or product demonstrations. Whatever content you choose, ensure it aligns with both your objectives and the needs of your audience. Additionally, tailor your content to the specific stage of the digital sales funnel. For example, when nurturing leads, focus on content that emphasizes your product's benefits and positions your brand as the market leader.

## 4. Different webinar types

**Panel:** These types of webinars allow you to have multiple people from your organization sharing their knowledge and expertise. You can even bring industry leaders to discuss their industry issues for lead generation purposes. This would be best for the top and middle of the funnel, where you're trying to acquire leads and demand for your products and services.

**Q&A:** This type of webinar is more interactive and engaging. One or more speakers from your organization will answer the questions that your audience asks. Q&A webinars are best when you're at the final stage trying to answer any lingering questions about your product. Also, this type of interaction is what creates an engaging webinar. Research has shown that 92% of viewers [xlii] want the webinar to end with a Q&A session, so you should incorporate this into all types of webinars.

**Interview:** This format typically has a presenter and an interviewer. It's best when you're trying to prove your expertise and knowledge at the top of the sales funnel.

**Single Individual Presenting:** This type of webinar is best when you are trying to share specific information, case studies, details about your product or service.

Each type of webinar is appropriate for a specific stage of the digital sales funnel and goal that you are trying to achieve. Choose the webinar style that will help you accomplish your goals.

## 5. Find Your Presenter

Choosing your presenter is a key step in the success of your webinar. Nothing ruins a webinar like a monotonous, uncharismatic speaker. In fact, recent research showed that 52% of people [xliii] said webinars were more enjoyable with a good presenter. A webinar provides personal interaction, allows you to build relationships with your buyers and attaches emotions to the decision-making process. It's well-known that emotions and mood affect consumer behaviour. [xliv] When you put your buyers in a positive mood, they're more likely to buy your product. Having a personable, enthusiastic, and charismatic presenter can make the webinar more engaging and leave a lasting impression.

## 6. Create Your Visual Aids

If you have chosen a single-person presentation format, then you need to create a PowerPoint. Ensure that you're keeping the visuals engaging and informative to keep your attendees' attention. If you choose another format, then you may want to create handouts or infographics that your audience can download or use to follow along with the presentation.

## 7. Determine the Time and Place

After you finish planning the webinar, decide when to air it. In general, research [xlv] has shown the middle of the week, from Tuesday to Thursday at 10-11 AM is the best time to host it. Also, you must determine the length of the webinar. If the webinar's too long,  you risk losing the engagement from your consumers. But if it's too short, it may not be viewed as valuable. It was found that 67% of registrations are for 60-minute webinars as opposed to only 8% for 30-minute webinars. Webinars that are one hour long are optimal.

When considering where you're going to host your webinar, make sure that you look at what technological capabilities you have, your budget and the different webinar services/software available to you.[xlvi]

## How to Maximize the Investment in Your Webinar

Creating a successful webinar for demand and lead generation doesn't end there. After planning and creating your company's webinar, it's essential to begin the promotion process to generate interest and gather participants.

## Promotion

When you're ready to promote the webinar, also create a webinar registration page with relevant, honest, and engaging information. You'll share this page in your promotions, so it should be user-friendly and peak your audience's curiosity. It's essential to provide accurate information on what your webinar will cover because if your attendees do not receive the value they thought they signed up for, you'll lose those leads.

Now you can begin promoting. How you choose to promote your webinar depends on a few factors. For example, your budget, the channels your target market is most active in and the stage of the digital sales funnel are important to consider. It's important to note that 59% of registrations [xlvii] occur less than a week before the webinar, so advertise extensively until that point in time.

There are four main advertising methods:

**Social Media.** This method is best when you are at the top of the funnel trying to generate demand and awareness about your product. Sharing your webinar information on social media will get the information out to a wider audience so that you can have more registration and attendance.

**Your Website.** Using your website allows you to target buyers that are already interested in and researching your company. This is best for the top and middle of the sales funnel.

**Email Campaign.** This is especially useful for the middle and end of the funnel. You can directly contact high-quality leads by using your current customer and prospect email list you generated when hosting past webinars. Email is effective and, in the past email has generated 57% of webinar registrations.[xlviii]

**Paid Advertising.** This is best for the top of the funnel when you are trying to generate awareness and demand. Paid advertising allows you to target specific audiences and have prime advertising placement. However, using some of the above free methods is better and still effective if you do not have the budget for paid advertising.


## Follow-Up

Congratulations – you promoted the webinar, generated lots of interest and finished hosting an amazing and informative webinar. But the work doesn't stop here. Following up is just as important for demand and lead generation as creating a good webinar. Following up with buyers at the top or middle of the funnel will help them progress to the next stage. If your buyers are at the bottom of the funnel, then following up will enhance their customer experience, keep you in communication with them and, ultimately, build more trust, loyalty, and sales.

### Here are 4 Things You Can Do in the Follow-Up Stage:

**Send a follow-up email to all registrants.** All registrants should receive a recording of the webinar. Be prepared to send a different email to those that attended and those that didn't. If you have a platform that tracks who stayed for the whole webinar, you can further segment your list and email sequences.

**Those that attended.** Thank your viewers for taking the time out of their day to participate in the webinar. If they attended the full webinar, encourage them to share and refer to it. If they hadn't seen the whole webinar, encourage them to go back and watch the replay. Also, at this time, you can share an offer, encourage them to book a meeting or demo, reply with questions, or whatever the next desired action you were hoping for from the webinar. Sharing a short feedback survey can help you understand what to improve on for future webinars.

**Those that didn't attend.** Send them an email encouraging them to watch the webinar. Share a webinar recording with an offer or call to action.

**Send follow up content.** If consumers have learned about your product and aren't ready to buy, then add them to a lead nurturing campaign. If your audience was at the top or middle of the funnel, you can send information for future or past webinars with similar topics. This is also a great time to share other blogs, whitepapers, or videos. You may want to provide a free trial, demo, or case study if they are in the middle or near the bottom of the sales funnel.

**Identify qualified leads.** Know who your ideal audience is and align your webinar to their pain points at the right stage of the funnel. Also, promote it across the right channels. Then, you've taken all the right steps in attracting your ideal audience. However, you may want to limit the number of registration form questions to encourage enrollment. You can't always tell how qualified a lead is from the registration form. There are additional ways to gather and determine a qualified sales opportunity.

**Gather more information to identify sales opportunities.** During the webinar, it's an opportunity to gather more information about your attendees and here's how:

**Take polls and ask questions** to get attendees to share more information about themselves. Ask about their pain points, industry, size of the company, etc., to narrow in on the most qualified for follow-up.

**Evaluate those most interested** to prioritize your follow-up focus on those more sales ready.

**Track those that attend** the full webinar versus those who partially attend or don't show.

## Ways to Improve Your Webinar

Analyze the data that you have gathered from your webinar. This can help you determine how to improve your results next time. The first important metric to look at is the attendance rate. Although it varies by industry, a rule of thumb is that 40%-50% of registrants [xlix] attendance is a good turn out. Next, look at how many of your prospects stayed until the end to see how much value the webinar added. An 80% retention rate [l] is good. Analyze the feedback survey you sent to registrants to address gaps. Then, review the questions you were asked during the webinar. This can help you determine if there was any content you needed to explain more in-depth. Also, review your promotions. For example, what media sources drove the highest registrants, and did you do any a/b testing against messaging and creative?

When used properly and created strategically, webinars are incredible tools for demand and lead generation and conversion. But webinars should not stand alone, and you should continue to produce other content. Using webinars in conjunction with blogs, whitepapers and other content types can make your digital sales funnel more effective.

## Use Influencers to Sell Your Products and Services

Influencer marketing is a newer type of marketing. One that can't be overlooked when looking to reach your potential buyers. Influencers are people with large followings on social media.  As strong brand ambassadors, companies negotiate with influencers to create and post content on their behalf. Compensation is usually based on the type of post and whether they're a micro or macro-influencer.

It is an effective strategy, as influencers are trusted by the company's target audience and can often influence shoppers to consider buying a business' product or service.

**Micro-Influencers:** a micro-influencer has between 1,000 to 100,000 followers on a specific platform.

**Macro-Influencers:** a macro-influencer has more than 100,000 followers. In most cases, these influencers tend to include internet and Hollywood celebrities. Due to their mass following, influencers tend to charge high prices for their services, and not usually targeted by small-to-mid size businesses.

The fact is influencers can have a real impact on your marketing and shouldn't be ignored. An influencer charges based on engagement. The costs will range based on the size of their following. Prices may vary from $20 to $1 million per post.

Here's a guide what to expect by platform[li]:

## Facebook ($25 /1,000 Followers)

Facebook is one of the largest social platforms with more than one billion daily users. This is a great channel for companies to reach consumers, and influencers are another tactic in your toolbox. The average cost per post is $25 per 1,000 followers and the price goes up from there.

Influencer post prices for Facebook:

- 10,000 followers could charge $250 per post
- 100,000 followers could charge $2,500 per post
- 1,000,000 followers could charge $25,000 per post

If you want an influencer to create a post with video content, they may charge an additional fee for creating the video. Or, if you invite an influencer to visit your location, they may ask you to cover their travel costs. For a streamlined influencer marketing experience, Facebook offers Brand Collabs Managers where you can connect and discuss your need and compare pricing between influencers. There's close to eight million influencers available through this tool.

## Instagram ($10 /1,000 Followers)

Instagram, which is owned by Facebook also has one billion users, many of which follow their favourite brand. Instagram is known to be the influencer hub and is a good place to start if you're looking to connect with influencers. The average price is $10 a post, per 1,000 followers. The price goes up with more followers.

Influencer post prices for Instagram:

- 10,000 followers could charge $100 per post
- 100,000 followers could charge $1,000 per post
- 1,000,000 followers could charge $10,000 per post

And, if you are looking for a celebrity connection, those influencers can cost up to $1 million dollars per post. Someone like Kylie Jenner, or Justin Bieber would fall into this category if they agreed to work with you.

## Twitter ($2/1,000 Followers)

Twitter features a smaller audience than Facebook with 330 million users. Although a smaller audience reach, it's a good platform to test as you won't pay as much to try it. Twitter influencers could charge as little as $2 per post, per 1,000 followers, one of the lowest prices to pay to engage with an influencer.

Influencer post prices for Twitter:

- 10,000 followers could charge $20 per post
- 100,000 followers could charge $200 per post
- 1,000,000 followers could charge $2,000 per post

## Snapchat ($10 /1,000 Followers)

Snapchat provides companies access to a range of influencers with over 188 million users. Influencers on Snapchat charge $10 per post, per 1,000 followers.

Influencer post prices for Snapchat:

- 10,000 followers could charge $100 per post
- 100,000 followers could charge $1,000 per post
- 1,000,000 followers could charge $10,000 per post

Unfortunately, Snapchat, doesn't let you see how many followers someone has. You can see a person's viewership on their Snapchat Story which might give you a sense of how big their following is.

The pricing model changes on Snapchat and goes by followers versus price per post.

A business will pay $10 per post, per 1,000 views. Like YouTube, Snapchat also offers a matchmaking program for companies and influencers.

## YouTube ($20 /1,000 Subscribers)

YouTube offers businesses access to a whole new set of influencers with more than 2.5 billion users in 2024. Influencers on YouTube may charge as little as $20 a video, per 1,000 subscribers.

Example of prices for influencer marketing on YouTube:

- 10,000 subscribers could charge $200 per video
- 100,000 subscribers could charge $2,000 per video
- 1,000,000 subscribers could charge $20,000 per video

Like Facebook, YouTube offers a platform for connecting with influencers, but it comes with a price. The platform FameBit[lii] matches influencers and companies. It uses several factors, like your budget, target audience, and goals, to connect you with an influencer. While it doesn't cost anything to join FameBit to find an influencer, the minimum project cost is $100.

## Blog ($60 /1,000 Visitors)

Many influencers write their own blogs. This is another way to connect with your target audience. You can pay for mentions in their blogs. This cost is around $60 per post, per 1,000 unique visitors to their blog page. Keep in mind pricing and results can differ by industry, topic, and length of the blog.

While more expensive than other platforms, blogs can deliver the best results. Blogs are 37% more effective[liii] for influencer marketing than other social media platforms like Facebook and YouTube.

There are many options available at varying price points to meet your budget. The best way to know if an influencer strategy is right for your business is to test it out. This might be the best performing tactic of all. Get with the times and give it a try.

Case Studies: Content Marketing and Lead Generation

## CONTENT MARKETING CASE STUDIES

## Dropbox – Simplifying Complex Concepts to Drive Conversion

**Background:** Dropbox, a cloud storage service, faced significant challenges in explaining its innovative concept to potential users who were unfamiliar with the idea of cloud storage. The complexity of the service created a barrier to user adoption, as many potential customers struggled to understand why they needed it.

**Strategy:** To overcome this challenge, Dropbox created a simple yet highly engaging explainer video. This video used clear visuals and straightforward language to demonstrate how Dropbox worked and the benefits it provided. The video was prominently featured on Dropbox's homepage, making it a central element of their marketing strategy.

**Results:** The explainer video played a crucial role in Dropbox's rapid growth. Within just 15 months, Dropbox's user base skyrocketed from 100,000 to over 4 million registered users. The video was instrumental in breaking down complex concepts and showcasing the value of Dropbox in a way that was easily understandable to the average user.

**Key Takeaways:** This case study highlights the importance of aligning your content with your audience's understanding and needs. By simplifying complex concepts and delivering them through engaging content, you can significantly boost conversion rates and drive rapid growth. For businesses, especially in the SaaS industry, this underscores the value of clear communication and strategic content planning as part of an integrated marketing plan.

## Drift – Building a Multi-Million Dollar Brand through Content Marketing

**Background:** Drift, a SaaS company specializing in conversational marketing, faced the challenge of building brand recognition and trust in a competitive market. To achieve rapid growth, they needed to establish themselves as a thought leader and drive customer engagement through strategic content marketing.

**Strategy:** Drift focused on a targeted content marketing strategy that leveraged specific audience segments. They developed a mix of educational content, such as blog posts, podcasts, and webinars, designed to resonate with their target audience. Additionally, Drift collaborated with industry influencers and partners to amplify their content's reach. They also adhered to SEO best practices to ensure their content was discoverable by potential customers.

**Results:** Through these efforts, Drift successfully transformed into a multi-million-dollar brand. Their content strategy not only increased brand awareness but also significantly boosted customer engagement and revenue. By focusing on delivering valuable content tailored to their audience's needs, Drift was able to establish a strong market presence and drive substantial business growth.

**Key Takeaways:** This case study illustrates the power of a well-defined content strategy in driving business success. By understanding their audience and leveraging content to address their needs, Drift was able to build a strong brand and achieve rapid growth. For SaaS companies, this case study highlights the importance of targeted content marketing as a key component of an effective and cost-efficient marketing strategy.

## LEAD GENERATION CASE STUDIES

## Boger Dental – Targeted Campaigns for High-Value Leads

Boger Dental, a dental practice, sought to attract potential patients for higher-margin services such as sedation dentistry, cosmetic dentistry, and dental implants. To achieve this, they created a targeted marketing campaign that optimized their website for conversions and utilized marketing automation to nurture leads. As a result, new patient appointments increased by 29%, and appointments for specialty services grew by 36%.

## Mira Clinic – Optimizing Lead Quality through A/B Testing

Mira Clinic, a Turkey-based cosmetic dentistry and plastic surgery clinic, ran a lead generation campaign using Facebook Lead Ads. They featured testimonial videos and conducted A/B testing with different optimization strategies. By focusing on conversion leads optimization, they were able to generate 48% more quality leads while reducing the cost per lead by 36%. This strategy allowed them to attract high-quality leads and improve the effectiveness of their marketing efforts.

These case studies illustrate the importance of targeted marketing strategies, optimization techniques like A/B testing, and the use of automation to improve lead quality and conversion rates. By applying these principles, businesses can achieve significant growth in their lead generation efforts.

**JUMPin2it Resources: Get the Insights You Need for Success**

At JUMPin2it, we provide the essential tools and knowledge to help you grow. Explore our library of resources, podcasts, events, and training to get what you need to move your business forward.

Visit: https://360integralmarketing.com/jump-in-2-it/

# JUMPin2it SECTION III - HOW TO GET A BETTER RETURN ON YOUR MARKETING DOLLARS

*"If you can't measure it, you can't improve it." Peter Drucker, Business Consultant*

## How to Measure Modern MROI

Many traditional marketers find themselves overwhelmed by digital speak, technology, quantitative methods, and artificial intelligence. Add modern marketing measurement ROI to the equation and it can be confusing.

Some marketing veterans are hesitant to tread into modern marketing. They believe technology, especially digital technology, has changed the fundamentals of marketing and unless you know HTML and Google Analytics, it's difficult to make headway.

Below is a summary of key considerations when looking to measure ROI in modern day marketing. Check your marketing efforts against these highlights and you might discover the new way to do marketing is like the old way but on technology steroids!

**Are you thinking like a CFO with numbers?** The investing metaphor is apt in that there are many different places where you can spend your money—countries, channels, products, and customer groups. How are you allocating your marketing dollars? The marketing discipline has evolved to where being quantitatively rigorous and having as much financial acumen as the CFO is now important.

**A crucial aspect of the process is the creation of test-and-learn discipline.** Testing anything means you need measurements. Everything measured is broken down into two elements: efficiency and effectiveness.

> **Efficiency:** consolidating the agency roster, running rigorous RFPs, negotiating commercial terms with all agencies, getting better at understanding costs and being very precise about competitively bidding out work.

> **Effectiveness:** improving targeting of digital media buys, understanding where best ROI, examining research activities to avoid duplication and to ensure building and sharing of knowledge.

**Measuring Modern Marketing ROI takes time:** unfortunately, test and learn projects or campaigns need time in market and can't be measured right way. Three to six months is a good length to determine its value and overall success.

**The captured savings goes into a pot** where it's measured and then redeployed to a series of growth projects. By reinvesting and continuing to test and learn, it will bring you added success and proven wins.

**The budget is now aligned, not on a percentage-of-sales basis,** but on a much more sophisticated, 'what-are-we-actually-getting-on-our-return' basis for that marketing spend.

## Back to Basics

It's basic, technology has helped marketing processes move faster and at a more granular level—both of which we wanted when we started out in marketing. Now we have this technology, so become friends with it and get back to the trenches. Deploy some math and finance skills to deliver your marketing solutions. One effective way is to take every marketing step you follow and re-imagine it with how technology and financial skills to do the same step. And you do not have to be a math or finance whiz for this, you only need somebody on your team who is and then ride the dragon.

# Modern Marketing Trends to Invest In

Whether you are a seasoned marketer or a senior executive, staying on top of modern ways to fill the sales funnel can be challenging. Furthermore, with new technology, preferences and buying patterns, how do you determine and prioritize your marketing investment?

Many of the basic principles for successful marketing haven't changed but how you get there and the tools to figure it out are continuously evolving.

## Basic Marketing Rule

Right message, to the right audience at the right time through the right channel drives the right response.

## Marketing Rule Adapted for the Times

The right sequence of touchpoints and messages across optimal channels, delivered to the right audience at the right time, drives the right sequence of responses to push your buyers down the sale funnel.

## Know Your ROMI

Wanting to figure out how your marketing dollars are working is not new. ROMI (Return on Marketing Investment) helps formalize marketing strategies and investments. And because of new tools, it's easier to track the buyers' journey and profitability.

### Data-Driving Marketing Strategy

The buyer being central to all your marketing efforts is why multiple channels and strategies need to come together to deliver a positive, cohesive brand experience to drive the right responses. A data-driven marketing strategy embraces today's tools to enable personalization, customization, and integration across platforms. Data needs to be shared across many business units, including Marketing, Sales, Finance and Customer Service to deliver a more complete view of the customer. Preferences, behaviour, demographics, values, and profitability data can then used to improve marketing effectiveness and to measure ROMI.

### Omnichannel Marketing

With a data-driven marketing strategy, it empowers omnichannel marketing. Omnichannel marketing provides a customer with a seamless experience across all interactions with your company's brand. It's why a strategy needs to fully-integrate the buyer's experience by uniting the experience from brick-and-mortar to browsing the web and anything in between. Commonly referred to as an omnichannel retail strategy approach to sales and marketing.

Multi-Touch Attribution (MTA) tracks and weighs in how each touch point leads to a sale or other action. This helps you better optimize content, campaigns, and channels to drive the best results. MTA determines the incremental impact of each ad, keyword phrase, downloaded whitepapers, videos or posts that attributed to the campaign's success, sale, or profitability of your business. There are many types of attribution models Bizable.com lists [liv] to start tracking marketing effectiveness.

## MarTech Stack

When running multiple campaigns and strategies it requires stackable Martech (marketing technology) that integrate for proper performance and management. Based on the size of your business, budget, and the complexity of your campaigns, the tools you'll need may vary.

# How to Measure a Brands Share of Voice

In the past, calculating the share of voice (SOV) was more of an approximation, where spend was estimated and competitor advertising often missed.

An accurate measurement methodology allows you to gauge where your brand stands and how to improve the effectiveness of your communication's strategy in the future.

Irrespective of the marketing mix, you need to focus on a calculation which involves a variation of the original share of voice formula:

**Your Brand Advertising / Total Market Advertising = Share of Voice**

With the newer avenues of SEO, PPC and Social Media, there are several tools that will calculate SOV and provide more accurate and regular updates.

Share of voice across social media platforms are tracked by the number of times your brand is mentioned on all statistically significant social media channels.

It's not advisable to track mentions of your brand manually, instead subscribe to some paid tools like Hootsuite, Sproutsocial, Brandwatch as they're cost effective and efficient in the long run.

To calculate organic search share of voice (SOV) manually:

**Brand Traffic/Total Market Traffic = Share of Voice** (data can be extracted from Google Analytics)

You can also get help from tools like Sysomos MAP, AdGooroo, SpyFu Recon, SpyFu Kombat, BrightEdge, Conductor, Google AdWords, Majestic SEO, Moz Open Site Explorer

Share of voice equivalent for PPC can be extracted from Google AdWords called Impression Share. This represents the percentage of times your ads were shown to users compared to the number of times your ads could've been shown, based on your keyword and campaign settings.

Having defined metrics and tools in place allows you to have a pulse on consumer preferences, as well as established competitors and new entries into the market that are gaining momentum. Your brand's success relies on a strong communications strategy and a feedback loop to ensure you stay current and effective.

## How to Measure Content Effectiveness

What doesn't get measured, doesn't get improved upon. Success needs to tie back to the business objectives and marketing goals. For tracking program success, measurement is extremely important. You'll need to list out how and when you measure efforts, the KPIs used and what success ultimately looks like.

### Metrics That Define Success

- Shared content, likes and comments
- Content downloads
- Contact Us requests (forms and inbound calls)

- Form completions for events, webinars, and gated content
- Website traffic, bounce rates and page views
- Sales volume, conversion rates, sales cycle, frequency, and profitability

Having the right resources to build out, distribute and measure your content will improve your ability to exceed your business and communications goals.



Google AdWords, Website Analytics, Facebook, LinkedIn, and Twitter all provide metrics to measure your performance. It depends on your communication objectives, but the more you can tie each step of engagement to the outcome, the better you'll measure performance. You may think content is subjective, but when content ties back to filling your sales funnel, it becomes more science than art.

## Ways to Lower Your Marketing Costs

To continue to evolve and grow a profitable business, you need to keep track of your costs to acquire, retain, and grow your customers' share of wallet. Here are three ways to lower your marketing costs:

1. Technology

Use marketing technology and automation platforms that integrate seamlessly with your other management systems. By choosing technology that coordinates across your business, you can gain a holistic view of the customer, streamline workflows, and potentially reduce manpower requirements. This approach not only saves time but also cuts down on operational costs.

## 2. Marketers on Demand

Consider hiring seasoned marketers on-demand, agencies, or consultants. These professionals require no training and can quickly step into their roles, reducing your go-to-market timeframe and keeping overhead costs down. Additionally, they bring fresh perspectives and expertise that can optimize your marketing efforts without the long-term commitment of full-time staff.

## 3. Outsource

Outsource digital marketing performance management to experts with the technical know-how your business needs. It's not practical—or cost-effective—to burden your internal marketing and IT resources with the complexities of digital management, tracking, and optimization. By partnering with specialists, you can achieve better results while maintaining the flexibility to scale as your business grows.

## The Value of Training and Consulting

Investing in targeted training and consulting services can further lower your marketing costs by enhancing your team's capabilities and refining your strategies. Training equips your team with the latest tools and techniques, reducing reliance on external help and improving overall efficiency. Consulting provides tailored advice that helps you avoid costly mistakes and optimize your marketing spend. Together, these resources empower your business to operate more effectively, cutting down on trial-and-error and enabling you to achieve better results with fewer resources.

---

Whether you implement any or all these strategies, there will always be factors beyond your control. However, by focusing on continuous improvement and leveraging external expertise, you can ensure your approach remains efficient and cost-effective. To grow your business, stay laser-focused on innovation, proactivity, and effectiveness in filling your sales funnel and keeping your customers happy.

**JUMPin2it Resources: Your Path to Success**

At JUMPin2it, we empower business owners and marketers with the tools and inspiration they need to succeed. Explore our resource library, podcasts, networking events, consulting, and training to ignite your growth and drive your business forward. Ready to take the leap? Dive into all that JUMPin2it has to offer.

Visit: https://360integralmarketing.com/jump-in-2-it/

# CONCLUSION

This guide empowers you to optimize the most effective strategies and tactics for your business without wasting valuable time and resources. However, skipping critical steps can be just as costly. Time isn't always on your side, and sometimes the key isn't waiting for perfection but ensuring that all essential steps are covered. The more holistically you understand your business and its role in the market, the better positioned you are to be prosperous.

Investing in training and consulting can be a game-changer, helping you avoid costly missteps and accelerate your growth. By equipping yourself and your team with the right skills and insights, you can navigate the complexities of marketing with greater confidence and efficiency. Sometimes, the smartest move is to act as the conductor, orchestrating the process, or to outsource key marketing strategies, tactics, and techniques to experts who can deliver results.

That's where JUMPin2it comes in. Through our podcasts, live events, training, and consultations, we provide the support and guidance you need to make things happen in your business. We help you bridge the gap between vision and action, ensuring that every step you take is strategic, effective, and aligned with your goals. With JUMPin2it, you're not just making a leap—you're making a leap toward lasting success.

## JUMPin2it: Where Vision Meets Action

At JUMPin2it, we're all about action—jumping into the challenges, opportunities, and strategies that drive real business success. Through our podcasts, live events, training, and consultations, we equip you to make the leap from vision to reality. Whether you're looking to grow, innovate, or refine your approach, we're here to guide and inspire every step of the way.

## Our Mission

To empower business owners by providing actionable insights and strategies through engaging podcasts, transformative live events, hands-on training, and expert consultations. We focus on helping you take decisive steps that make things happen in your business.

## Why JUMPin2it?

With Gabrielle and Anita at the helm, JUMPin2it is more than a source of advice—it's a catalyst for action. Our live events energize and connect business owners, fostering a community where ideas are shared, and momentum is built. Our training sessions and consultations provide practical, results-oriented strategies tailored to your unique business needs.

## Passion-Driven Success

We're driven by a passion for helping business owners leap into action. Our podcasts deliver inspiring stories and expert insights that push you to take bold steps. Our live events and training sessions are crafted to build your confidence and skill set, ensuring you're equipped to implement effective strategies. And through personalized consultations, we help you fine-tune these strategies to achieve your business goals.

## Your Path to Success

At JUMPin2it, we believe in taking bold steps toward business success. Our podcasts, events, training, and consultations are designed to help you navigate the complexities of running a business with clarity and confidence. We're here to ensure that every leap you take is grounded in solid strategy and supported by actionable insights.

Jump into action with JUMPin2it, and let's make things happen together. Your success isn't just our mission—it's our inspiration.

## JUMPin2it: Your Path to Success Begins with a Discovery Call

At JUMPin2it, we believe every journey to success starts with a conversation. Schedule a discovery call today to uncover the personalized strategies your business needs. From there, explore our resource library, podcasts, networking events, consulting, and training to ignite your growth and propel your business forward. Ready to take the leap? Start with a call and dive into all that JUMPin2it has to offer.

Visit: https://360integralmarketing.com/jump-in-2-it/

# FOOTNOTES

---

[i] https://hbr.org/2014/10/the-value-of-keeping-the-right-customers

[ii] https://www.forbes.com/sites/forbesagencycouncil/2018/01/16/why-integrated-marketing-needs-to-be-the-foundation-of-your-b2b-strategy/?sh=6a55b6ca6eff

[iii] https://www.forbes.com/sites/allbusiness/2019/05/24/b2b-sales-tips/?sh=3aa2c338329d

[iv] https://www.hubspot.com/marketing-statistics

[v] https://www.bluecorona.com/blog/b2b-marketing-statistics/

[vi] https://www.prmoment.com/pr-research/integrated-campaigns-are-31-percent-more-effective-at-building-brands-according-to-research#:~:text=SUBSCRIBE-,Integrated%20campaigns%20are%2031%25%20more%20effective,building%20brands%2C%20according%20to%20research&text=Two%2Dthirds%20of%20consumers%20think,research%20firm%20Kantar%20Millward%20Brown.

vii https://www.edelman.com/research/2020-b2b-thought-leadership-impact-study

viii https://www.emailmonday.com/marketing-automation-statistics-overview/

ix https://www.uberflip.com/snapapp/

x https://chiefmartec.com/2017/05/marketing-techniology-landscape-supergraphic-2017/

xi https://blog.marketo.com/2015/08/marketo-data-tells-us-what-is-the-top-conversion-rate-by-channel.html

xii https://support.google.com/google-ads/answer/6324971?hl=en

xiii https://support.google.com/google-ads/answer/6324971?hl=en

xiv https://support.google.com/google-ads/answer/2545661?hl=en#:~:text=Remarketing%20lists%20are%20created%20by,Viewed%20certain%20videos xv https://www.youtube.com/ads/how-it-works/?subid=ca-en-ha-yt-bk-c-plt!o3~Cj0KCQjwl4v4BRDaARIsAFjATPkNNLXRKiI9AVidQxt0muNpcwmyJesNiGemSfox39bq6mHW-Xu5AigaAkUhEALw_wcB~%7Badgroup%7D~kwd-31647562193~1697079281~329899190535

xvi https://support.google.com/google-ads/answer/2497941?hl=en

xvii https://www.reliablesoft.net/facebook-statistics/

xviii https://business.instagram.com/blog/targeting-instagram-ads/

xix https://backlinko.com/facebook-users

xx https://videos.brightedge.com/research-report/BrightEdge_ChannelReport2019_FINAL.pdf

xxi https://videos.brightedge.com/research-report/BrightEdge_ChannelReport20
_FINAL.pdf

xxii https://sparktoro.com/blog/2018-search-market-share-myths-vs-realities-of-google-bing-amazon-facebook-duckduckgo-more/

xxiii https://videos.brightedge.com/research-report/BrightEdge_ChannelReport2019_FINAL.pdf

xxiv https://ahrefs.com/blog/long-tail-keywords/

xxvhttps://www.wordstream.com/serp#:~:text=Search%20engine%20results%20pages%20are,presents%20them%20with%20a%20SERP.

xxvi https://www.semrush.com/

xxvii https://blog.hubspot.com/marketing/2013-inbound-marketing-stats-charts?__hstc=23038436.9d881d6a21677a487a607d3f8abcce0c.1413345670760.1413345670760.1413345670760.1&__hssc=23038436.1.1413345670772&__hsfp=266759377

xxviii https://www.searchenginejournal.com/seo-101/seo-statistics/

[xxix] https://searchengineland.com/search-sends-more-better-traffic-to-content-sites-than-social-media-study-says-72988

[xxx] https://www.searchenginejournal.com/seo-101/seo-statistics/

[xxxi] https://searchengineland.com/eye-tracking-study-everybody-looks-at-organic-listings-but-most-ignore-paid-ads-on-right-67698

[xxxii] https://convertwithcontent.com/seo-vs-ppc-which-is-better-for-my-business/

[xxxiii] https://www.coredna.com/blogs/ecommerce-trends#2

[xxxiv] https://www.on24.com/blog/why-webinar-marketing-fuels-demand-generation-in-2019/

[xxxv] https://www.on24.com/blog/why-webinar-marketing-fuels-demand-generation-in-2019/

[xxxvi] https://99firms.com/blog/webinar-statistics/

xxxvii https://outgrow.co/blog/statistics-on-webinars


xxxviii https://www.inc.com/logan-chierotti/harvard-professor-says-95-of-purchasing-decisions-are-subconscious.html

xxxix https://www.quicksprout.com/webinar-conversions/#:~:text=The%20conversion%20rate%20of%20webinars%20is%20insane%3A%20Say%2C,on%20the%20price%20and%20a%20few%20other%20factors.


xl https://www.quicksprout.com/webinar-conversions/#:~:text=The%20conversion%20rate%20of%20webinars%20is%20insane%3A%20Say%2C,on%20the%20price%20and%20a%20few%20other%20factors.


xli https://www.convinceandconvert.com/digital-marketing/create-a-webinar/


xlii https://outgrow.co/blog/statistics-on-webinars


xliii https://outgrow.co/blog/statistics-on-webinars


xliv https://smart-retailer.com/putting-your-customers-in-a-buying-mood/

xlv https://blog.gotomeeting.com/7-webinar-benchmarks-every-marketer-should-know/

xlvi https://www.ventureharbour.com/webinar-software-10-best-webinar-platforms-compared/

xlvii https://blog.gotomeeting.com/7-webinar-benchmarks-every-marketer-should-know/

xlviii https://blog.gotomeeting.com/7-webinar-benchmarks-every-marketer-should-know/

xlix https://outgrow.co/blog/statistics-on-webinars

l https://www.convinceandconvert.com/digital-marketing/converting-your-webinar-audience/

li https://www.webfx.com/influencer-marketing-pricing.html#influencer-pricing-platform

lii https://support.google.com/youtube/answer/9385307?hl=en

liii https://www.digitalmarketing.org/blog/how-much-does-influencer-marketing-cost

liv https://www.bizible.com/blog/marketing-attribution-models-complete-list

**Gabrielle Hailmann and Anita Booth**

# JUMPin2it! BREAKTHRU
# MARKETING GUIDE